Direct Marketing

Marketing in Action Series
Series Editor: Norman Hart

Lively and 'easy to read', each book in the 'Marketing in Action' series is a clear, concise, action-oriented and up-to-date summary of a specific marketing topic. The books avoid jargon and provide busy marketers with valuable, practical step-by-step guidance. Ideal for marketers in organisations of any size, the books will also appeal to students studying for formal qualifications in marketing (CIM, CAM).

In producing this series, the advice and assistance has been sought of a prestigious editorial panel representing the principal professional bodies, trade associations and business schools.

The Series Editor for the Marketing in Action books is Norman Hart who is a writer of some ten books himself. He currently runs his own marketing consultancy, and is also an international lecturer on marketing, public relations and advertising at conferences and seminars.

Already available in the series:

A Practical Guide to Integrated Marketing Communications
Tom Brannan

How to Produce Successful Advertising
David Farbey

Successful Product Management
Stephen Morse

Getting the Best from Agencies
Geoffrey Smith

The Effective Use of Sponsorship
David Wragg

Creating Effective Marketing Communications
Daniel Yadin

Relationship Marketing
Merlin Stone and Neil Woodcock

Strategic Marketing Planning and Evaluation
Geoff Lancaster and Lester Massingham

Forthcoming titles in the series are:

Branding
Geoffrey Randall

Introduction to Marketing
Geoff Lancaster and Paul Reynolds

Marketing a Service
Ian Ruskin-Brown

Sales and Sales Management
Chris Horsman

International Marketing
Keith Lewis and Matthew Housden

Available from all good bookshops, or to obtain further information please contact the publishers at the address below:

Kogan Page Ltd
120 Pentonville Road
London N1 9JN
Tel: 0171 278 0433
Fax: 0171 837 6348

Direct
Marketing

Margaret Allen

Series Editor: Norman Hart

**KOGAN
PAGE**

First published in 1997

Apart from any fair dealing for the purposes of research or private study, or criticism or review, as permitted under the Copyright, Designs and Patents Act, 1988, this publication may only be reproduced, stored or transmitted, in any form or by any means, with the prior permission in writing of the publishers, or in the case of reprographic reproduction in accordance with the terms and licences issued by the CLA. Enquiries concerning reproduction outside those terms should be sent to the publishers at the undermentioned address:

Kogan Page Limited
120 Pentonville Road
London N1 9JN

© Margaret Allen, 1997

The right of Margaret Allen to be identified as author of this work has been asserted by her in accordance with the Copyright, Designs and Patents Act 1988.

British Library Cataloguing in Publication Data
A CIP record for this book is available from the British Library.

ISBN 0 7494 2052 9

Typeset by Intype London Ltd
Printed and bound in Great Britain by Biddles Ltd, Guildford and Kings Lynn

Contents

Chapter 1   **What is Direct Marketing?**   **9**
Direct marketing defined   9
What is the future for direct marketing?   11
How much is spent on direct marketing?   12
Who is spending in direct marketing?   14
The tools of direct marketing   14
A new approach to direct marketing   18

Chapter 2   **What has Caused the Rapid Growth
in Direct Marketing?**   **21**
Technological developments   21
Media fragmentation   23
The growth of integrated communications   27

Chapter 3   **The Facts and Figures of Direct Mail**   **38**
What is direct mail?   38
Growth of direct mail   38
Who sends direct mail?   39
The consumer sector   42
What do consumers do with direct mail?   44
What does the business-to-business sector do with
direct mail?   45
Attitudes to direct mail   46

Chapter 4   **How to Get a Direct Mail Campaign Started**   **51**
Who will be responsible for producing the work?   52
Planning procedures to get your campaign off the
ground   56
Guidelines on having the work produced   58
Optimising external working relationships   60

Chapter 5   **The Direct Mail Creative Package**   **63**
Timing plans   63
Creative brief   63
Producing the creative package   64

	Elements of a direct mail campaign	65
	Guidelines on producing effective letters	68
	Assessing the creative package	72
	The production process	72
	How much does all this cost?	75
Chapter 6	**Mailing Lists and Database Management**	**77**
	Mailing lists	77
	Database management	87
Chapter 7	**Direct Response Advertising**	**91**
	Direct response television advertising	93
	Direct response press advertising	95
	Direct response radio advertising	97
Chapter 8	**Telemarketing**	**100**
	Inbound telemarketing	101
	Outbound telemarketing	105
	Customer care lines	107
	Telephone preference service	107
Chapter 9	**Mail Order and Direct Selling**	**109**
	Mail order – traditional	109
	Mail order – new generation	112
	Direct selling	113
	Future developments in home shopping	115
Chapter 10	**Door-to-door**	**117**
	What is to be delivered?	118
	To whom is it to be delivered?	119
	How is it to be delivered?	119
	What checks should be made to validate delivery?	120
	How much will it cost?	121
Chapter 11	**Research Techniques in Direct Marketing**	**122**
	Developing creative material	122
	Analysing creative material in test markets	124
	Post-campaign analysis	125
Chapter 12	**New Marketing Communication Opportunities**	**128**
	The Internet	128
	Compact disc technology	133
	Interactive kiosks	134
	Interactive television	134

Appendix   136
Recommended Further Reading   138

Index   *139*

Chapter 1

What is Direct Marketing?

Since it was first formally 'invented' some time in the 1950s, direct marketing as an area of promotional communication now appears to be coming of age.

Direct marketing is not an entirely new marketing tool. Elements of direct marketing have been established for many years; the infamous door-to-door salesman being a case in point. What has happened to direct marketing over the years is that it has grown in both 'depth' and 'breadth' as an area of promotional communication. This growth in depth has been driven directly by the advent of new technologies which enable increasingly sophisticated techniques to be used both to find and to communicate with potential customers. Along with the growth of the technology there has been an increase in the breadth of techniques employed in this field of direct communication.

Over the years, many textbooks have been written about direct marketing. Most leading companies either claim to be using it or intend to use it in the near future. Communication specialists are often heard waxing lyrical about the advantages that direct marketing potentially offers; benefits that were only previously dreamt of – that of reaching increasingly elusive customers directly without any apparent wastage. But what exactly is direct marketing?

DIRECT MARKETING DEFINED

If a typical member of the public is asked to define direct marketing, after a look of disbelief and a blank expression, he or she may be coaxed eventually into volunteering that it is 'junk mail', which, of course, they never read and wish would stop. Until fairly recently, this was also the response that would be given by many marketing departments in companies both large and small. The tide, however, is now starting to turn as companies begin to realise the breadth of this area of marketing communications and above all the potential advantages it can bring them.

The potential of this communication area spreads far beyond direct mail; although this is the most familiar and perhaps the most visible of the communication techniques which make up the full remit of direct marketing. But it is only part of the full story. Companies which are involved now and in the future with marketing and communicating with customers need to be aware of and familiar with all the direct marketing communication tools that are potentially available.

The official definition of direct marketing by the Direct Marketing Association is that it is:

> **Communications where data are used systematically to achieve quantifiable marketing objectives, where direct contact is invited or made between a company and its customers and prospective customers.**

This definition is very worthy and sets out the scope, features and some of the parameters of direct marketing. However, it stops short of explaining fully the *benefits* that direct marketing can bring. A more complete, albeit more wordy, definition is that:

> **Direct marketing is any form of one-to-one communication with potential customers. The ultimate objective of using any of these promotional tools will be to effect a sale but much of the communication will be to keep open a *dialogue* that is vital in long term *relationship building*.**

Two areas of benefit in this definition that set it apart and explain the real and potentially longer term benefits of direct marketing are worthy of discussion. They are 'dialogue' and 'relationship building'.

It is the establishment of a *dialogue* which is perhaps least understood and perhaps the most feared as it does not always show an immediate payback in terms of 'boxes moved off shelves'. Consider, for example a car manufacturer who is committed to a programme of direct marketing – it would be naïve to expect an immediate upturn in sales after one mailshot. Rather, direct marketing will be viewed as a long-term investment that will help to secure the car manufacturer a position on the mental 'shopping list' when a potential customer is next in the market for a new car.

Likewise, *relationship building* is one of those 'in' marketing terminologies that is regularly bandied around by communication specialists. Once achieved, you have built a bridge to your customer that will help to instil loyalty in the long term. Relating back to the car manufacturer, through regular communication a relationship can be built that could lead ultimately to a commitment to purchase.

Advertising specialists, and advertising agencies in particular, are firm believers and proponents of the philosophy that it is only through highly visible above-the-line communication techniques that dialogue/relationship building can occur. This above-the-line communication in turn leads to a franchise being built and maintained with a potential customer.

Above-the-line advertising is undeniably potent and has an impressive track record of success. Also true about advertising is that it is extremely expensive, and its audiences are fragmenting and becoming increasingly difficult to locate and track.

> Above-the-line communication techniques are essential to build up and maintain a relationship with potential customers.

Marketing departments are now beginning to question the role that they see their advertising playing versus that which their agency desires. There has always been a healthy degree of tension in the advertising 'sell' versus 'art' debate, but in the recent past, marketing departments have become more sceptical regarding the role their advertising agencies see their work fulfilling – many advertising agencies appear to have forgotten that their advertisements are there to sell.

This shift in attitude is highlighted by findings of a survey in the trade magazine *Media & Marketing Europe*. The number of clients who rate creativity as the most important factor in choosing an agency has fallen dramatically, from 90 per cent in 1994 to 50 per cent in 1995. Peter Slater, Vice President Marketing for Nissan Europe, sums up this ground swell of opinion: 'The agency will say that creativity is the most important thing, but obviously to us an increase in sales is more eloquent.'

The coincidence of this questioning ground swell of opinion against advertising along with the fragmentation of media usage patterns and advances in technology mean that marketing departments are rightly re-examining their approach to communication with customers. Only through such questioning will they be satisfied that they are optimising the potential of their promotional pound.

WHAT IS THE FUTURE FOR DIRECT MARKETING?

The time is now right for direct marketing to seize this opportunity to ensure that it is given a role as an integral part of the communication mix. It is unique because effectively it counteracts many of the negatives associated with above-the-line advertising – it is truly accountable. Marketers are able to have quantifiable results and hence reassurance that their communications are delivering as intended.

The best scenario will involve direct marketing being poised to become *the* communication tool of the future which will have the greatest chance of delivering an effective targeted sales message with the minimum of wastage. The worst scenario is still rosy because it will leave direct marketing recognised as an integral element in the communication mix that brings a unique set of strengths that cement relationships with clients to achieve sales.

Similarly, in the business-to-business field there has always been a certain degree of dissatisfaction with the dedicated use of above-the-line techniques. Advertising via the consumer media always resulted in some wastage, whereas advertisements placed in the specialist press, while highly targeted, can give limited coverage. As budgets in the business-to-business field are often more limited than those in the consumer field, it is even more crucial that wastage is kept to a minimum. This is where direct marketing techniques show themselves to be ideal tools.

The trend towards direct marketing is already starting to establish itself. Recent research from Datamonitor Publications indicates that the expenditure growth rate of direct marketing has far outstripped that of advertising. This research indicates that over the period 1990–94, total above-the-line advertising grew by 1.4 per cent in comparison with the growth of direct marketing of 2.16 per cent.

HOW MUCH IS SPENT ON DIRECT MARKETING?

As there is currently a dearth of standardised information that covers both above- and below-the-line spending, data from a variety of sources needs to be studied to understand the overall picture of what is happening to total communication spending in the UK.

The data in Table 1.1 highlights the size of direct mail expenditure in comparison with above-the-line expenditure

From this data, which features only one element of direct marketing – direct mail – the picture looks relatively healthy, with direct mail expenditure accounting for more than that allocated to outdoor, radio and cinema combined in 1995. Direct mail is still apparently dwarfed by the massive spends on both press and television. These figures, however, grossly underestimate the impact of direct marketing in its totality.

Table 1.1 *UK Advertising Expenditure 1994*

Medium	£ million	% Spend
Press	5,979	54.6
Television	3,103	28.3
Direct mail	1,135	10.4
Outdoor	378	3.4
Radio	296	2.7
Cinema	69	0.6
Total	10,960	100

Source: Advertising Association Yearbook/DMIS

A more complete picture emerges on examination of data supplied by the Direct Marketing Association whose census of the direct marketing industry, conducted in conjunction with the Henley Centre, indicated that the total expenditure in 1995 was in excess of £5.5 billion.

A breakdown of the areas of expenditure in direct marketing are included in Table 1.2.

Table 1.2 *Direct Marketing Expenditure Breakdown*

Direct Marketing Tool	Expenditure £ millions
Direct mail	1,135
National press display ads	786
National magazine ads	616
Regional display ads	325
Direct response TV	398
Direct response radio	47
Posters/outdoor	45
Cinema	2
Inserts	214
Telemarketing	1,175
Contract magazines	22
Door-to-door	233
Inserts	216
New media	50
Total	5,598

Source: Direct Marketing Association Research Centre

This breakdown highlights that the major areas of expenditure are direct mail and telemarketing. However, if all media-based direct marketing was combined, this would be the largest category with an expenditure of about £2200 million.

WHO IS SPENDING IN DIRECT MARKETING?

A brief glance over the membership of the Direct Marketing Association
(DMA) reads more like the *Who's Who* in UK industry and commerce.
Membership is broken down into advertisers, agencies, list and database
suppliers, and mailing houses and suppliers. The advertisers are represented from all areas of industry: financial services, charities,
telecommunications, the media, catalogues, automotive, retail, etc. Names
mentioned include Barclays Bank, RSPB, Mercury Communications,
Sainsbury, ITV Association, Empire Stores, Great Universal Stores, Volks-
wagen. While being representative, it is not a totally comprehensive list
of UK industry, because up to July 1996 there are only 196 members.
Copies of this list are available from the DMA whose address is contained
in the Appendix.

If direct mail, being the largest category of direct marketing, is used as
an indicator of the use and users of direct marketing, analysis of the
information supplied by the Direct Mail Information Service reveals some
interesting facts:

❏ Two-thirds of the top 3000 advertisers in the UK now have an individual responsible for direct mail.
❏ One-third of total advertising expenditure is spent on direct mail, in
  the top 3000 companies who have someone responsible for direct mail.
❏ 61 per cent of users of direct mail and 68 per cent of potential users
  claimed that direct mail would become more important in the next
  five years.
❏ 80 per cent of the top 1500 UK advertisers use direct response advertising.

Direct marketing for many companies already appears to be a major force
in the communication mix and this is at a time when many companies
have not yet used it as a promotional tool.

THE TOOLS OF DIRECT MARKETING

The techniques referred to in Table 1.2 are indicative of the majority of
the techniques that are available for use. In this book, however, a few extra
techniques will be discussed that may be of importance in the future.

Definitions of the techniques that make up the field of direct marketing
differ greatly. The scope covered in this book is deliberately broader than
many, but is judged to be a realistic and comprehensive approach to

indicate how direct marketing can be used in communication plans. Individual chapters provide more detail on the techniques.

The field of direct marketing comprises:

❏ Direct mail – consumer and business-to-business.
❏ Media-based, direct response advertisements – TV, press and radio.
❏ Telemarketing – in- and out-bound calls
❏ Mail order and direct selling.
❏ Door-to-door.
❏ New media – the Internet, CD Rom, multimedia kiosks, video on demand, interactive television.

A brief description of these techniques follows.

Direct mail

Direct mail is the method used to reach identified prospects and existing customers through personally addressed advertising which is delivered through the post at home or to a business address.

There is still some confusion between direct mail and unaddressed communications which are received through the letter-box. Door-to-door communication in the form of leaflets, letters, samples, etc is not addressed personally and can only be targeted at a postal sector, not at individual homes or consumers. Admittedly, door-to-door targeting has become more sophisticated recently as it has benefited from the learning of database management as applied to direct mail proper. This activity is judged to be a subsector of direct mail; its marginally less sophisticated cousin.

The development of the creative package that comprises a direct mail-shot is critical to its success. The creative package can comprise any number of elements, although at its most basic it is an envelope, letter and reply device. Many additional elements are now included in direct mail-shots and care must be taken to ensure that they are appropriate. The consumer is becoming more and more direct mail literate so every attempt must be made to optimise the package to achieve its objectives. Research techniques, both qualitative and quantitative, are increasingly employed to help in this development stage.

Even with the most effective and innovative mailing package, it would be rendered completely useless without an effective database. Database compilation and management techniques are a burgeoning industry whose growth has been initiated and fuelled by the advent of computer technology that enables large amounts of data to be handled, processed and sorted quickly and accurately. Without computer-based technology, the direct mail industry would not have been able to grow in the way that it has. Manual administration of a direct mail campaign using a card index system, for example, would be too labour-intensive to be economic.

Thanks to computer-based technology, an effective database enables an appropriate mail-shot to be posted to the target audience.

In summary, the direct mail technique relies on an appropriate mail-shot being posted to the target audience which is usually located through the use of a database.

Media-based direct response advertising

This area of direct marketing has grown rapidly in recent years. It comprises all advertisements which have a response mechanism built into them in the form of a freepost address or, more frequently, a telephone number. They are widely used on TV, in the press and, to a lesser degree, on commercial radio. The reasons for the growth in this form of direct marketing are twofold: technological advances and the marketers' desire to measure reliably the efficacy of their communications. This direct approach to advertising is not new as many companies have used successfully services such as freepost reply devices for many years.

Technological advances in telecommunications and, in its turn, telemarketing have, however, fuelled the growth of this technique. The ability of exchanges and handling houses to cope with a large volume of calls simultaneously enables advertisers to use this form of direct communication. These techniques give the advertiser instant feedback to judge whether an advertisement has been successful or not. It has obvious appeal to the advertiser but, owing to the instantaneous nature of this accountability, it can be less than popular with some advertising agencies who may feel intimidated.

Direct response advertising is a technique that has grown spectacularly and is likely to be of increasing importance in the future. Many advertisers use this at the start of their direct marketing campaign as a method of establishing a database.

Telemarketing

This is another area that has grown as a result of the advent of modern technology. It is usually viewed as having two separate functions: that of making outbound calls and that of receiving inbound calls.

The use of outbound calls as a method of marketing often comes in for much criticism in the consumer market as it is judged by many to be too intrusive. As a method of business-to-business communication, it does have more worth and for some companies it is a vital element in their communication package.

Inbound calls is the area of telemarketing which has experienced the greatest rate of growth in both consumer and business-to-business fields. Its growth, as previously discussed, has gone hand-in-hand with the growth of media-based direct response advertising. It has great appeal for the customer and advertiser alike owing to the immediacy of response and action. This is further enhanced through the use of freephone or low-call tariff numbers which encourage potential customers to make a call as they do not feel that they are being financially penalised for making contact.

Mail order

Mail order is not a new direct marketing tool. Many catalogues, which were introduced in the 19th century, have formed the basis of some of today's retailers – eg, Sears. The major players in traditional catalogues are established successfully and are among some of the major users of direct mail. They are likely to continue to play a significant role in the UK retailing scene.

The major development in the catalogue/mail order sector has been the advent of more specialist and targeted mail order offerings. This increase in choice and often quality is helping to change slowly the shape of the mail order industry in the UK. This trend is already established in the USA and, as a result, some of their more successful operators are crossing the Atlantic in pursuit of new business over here – eg, Racing Green. This is likely to be an area of increasing commercial importance in the future.

Direct selling

This grouping of direct marketing techniques forms a loose alliance which brings goods directly into customers' homes without the intervention of an established delivery or distribution system. They are sold via single or multi-level sales networks or party plans. Within each category there are large and small operators – Avon, for example, is one of the world's largest cosmetic companies and operates via direct selling. Goods as diverse as Tupperware and Ann Summers underwear are sold via party plans. Multi-level or pyramid selling and related techniques have been responsible for fuelling the growth of companies such as Amway. These categories may be viewed as being more on the periphery of direct marketing, but they warrant inclusion and discussion as potential selling techniques.

Door-to-door

This is a close relation of direct mail in that areas are targeted where it is believed receptive potential customers may live. They receive promotional literature through their doors which may help to stimulate a purchase. The key difference between door-to-door and direct mail is that it is non-personalised.

New media

These techniques demonstrate the dynamism and speed of change in the area of direct marketing. They present the marketer with the greatest challenge because they are an unknown entity. Marketers who decide to use them will have to go through a steep learning curve to ensure that they are used appropriately and that they offer measurable benefits that go beyond the 'hype'.

The new media is a diverse area that covers channels such as the Internet, which claims to have access to millions of people on a worldwide basis. The efficacy of the Internet as a worldwide direct marketing tool is as yet largely unproven, but its potential, if appropriately harnessed, is undeniable.

Other developments in the area of direct communication through kiosks, interactive TV and video are still in their infancy, but again are methods that could force the marketer to re-evaluate the approach taken in direct marketing.

The CD-Rom is established in the area of games and home computers, but its relevance as a direct marketing tool is largely unproven.

It is acknowledged that owing to their current novelty, the use of any of the new media techniques tools involves a degree of risk. They are worthy of discussion as potential benefits could be gained for businesses which are among the first to learn about and use them.

Companies which are the first to use the new media techniques may gain the advantage over their competitors.

A NEW APPROACH TO DIRECT MARKETING

For the information in this book to be of use, changes may need to be made to the way that direct marketing is thought about. Many companies think of direct marketing as just another communication tool that can be slotted into their marketing plans. They commit to trying it out for a year to see how it goes. This approach is totally erroneous. To reap all the potential benefits of direct marketing, a long-term perspective must be taken.

Four distinct phases are involved in setting up and bringing a successful and fully fledged direct marketing programme to the market. Irrespective of the individual tools selected for a direct marketing programme, the thinking and planning procedure that should be taken is identical. If companies are unable or unwilling to follow this approach, their campaigns are unlikely to be successful in the long term.

The recommended approach is one that may already be familiar: it is similar to finding an ideal partner for life. The phases in thinking that must be gone through are as follows.

Phase 1: Exploring the alternatives

If direct marketing is a new technique with which a company is largely unfamiliar, it will be at the exploratory stage. This uncertainty may make a company feel that it is not up-to-date with the new techniques. It will be aware that much has been written about direct marketing in the trade press and that many companies are claiming to use it or are already using it.

The many techniques of direct marketing now need to be appraised to isolate those that could be the most appropriate. This book provides the base knowledge for this appraisal to be conducted.

If direct marketing is already part of communication plans, a reappraisal of alternative techniques still needs to be done because new methods and approaches to direct marketing are presenting themselves every day. This area of communication is still in its infancy, but it is developing and evolving fast. Companies must never stop looking at and appraising the alternatives as they present themselves.

Phase 1 is complete when an opinion regarding which tool or tools could best suit the market situation is formulated. The company is now ready to enter into a 'relationship'.

Phase 2: Avoiding the 'one-night stand'

The company's management is now convinced of the benefits that can be gained from using direct marketing and a budget has been allocated to develop a campaign. At this stage, they must start to plan far ahead, preparing plans not just for year one, but for years three, five, and even ten. They must demonstrate their commitment to this area of communication. If they cannot demonstrate or receive the backing for a long-term approach, they may be disappointed ultimately with these techniques. All

A long-term approach must be adopted to bring a successful direct marketing programme to the market.

of the rewards are not immediate. Always be cautious when planning and try not to over-promise on expected results. Methods of analysing the results of direct marketing campaigns will be discussed fully in Chapter 11.

Having passed this stage, management will have crossed one of the major hurdles over which many marketing departments have stumbled and, as a result, will have killed off many fledgling campaigns in their infancy.

Phase 3: The 'courtship'

The company's campaign is up and running, and the experiences are still fairly new, heady and exciting. Management must try to remain level-headed about early successes and failures. At this stage the knowledge base about their customers and what they are expecting should be maximised. Communication techniques and approaches to handling the database are still being perfected. This is optimised through research and database management techniques which will be discussed in more detail in Chapters 11 and 6 respectively.

Phase 4: The 'marriage'

If this stage is reached in a direct marketing campaign, the rewards of the work that has been put into building the relationship with customers will now start to be reaped. The danger area at this stage is, as in a real marriage, that 'familiarity breeds contempt'. The familiar should not be accepted as the norm; rather, new ways of improving and enhancing relationships with customers should be sought. It is only through such constant reviewing of communication techniques and approach that a relationship with customers will be a long and fruitful one. If complacency does take over, then sadly, the result can result in divorce because the campaign will stop delivering effectively.

This approach in thinking is not intended to be glib. Only through approaching the use of direct marketing with this framework and learning curve in mind will companies be assured of a greater chance of success with their communication campaigns.

The world of direct marketing is littered with examples of companies which did not follow this approach. Many have flitted in and out without showing a long-term commitment, while others have never let their relationship grow beyond the one-night stand – a quick sale and bye bye! Sadly, many started promisingly but stopped trying, with the result that their compaigns were hackneyed and under-performed.

Chapter 2

What has Caused the Rapid Growth in Direct Marketing?

There are two unrelated phenomena which, while separate, have had the combined effect of prompting the meteoric rise of direct marketing as a communication tool: first, technological developments and secondly, the fragmentation of media which lead to a desire for an alternative, more accountable communications medium.

TECHNOLOGICAL DEVELOPMENTS

It is not intended to go into great depth to explain the complexities of the technological innovation that has fuelled the growth in direct marketing; suffice it to say that it is an area of rapid and continuous change that has enabled the following processes to become possible.

Data handling

Computers have enabled large quantities of data to be stored and processed more quickly and accurately than an equivalent manual process. Direct mail would be a far less feasible option without computers.

Software developments

Software packages to aid the data handling process are an indispensable tool. Technology is available to handle a direct mail campaign from the simple through to the more complex. The entry price for these software packages at around £100 makes it affordable to even the smallest company. Additional bolt-on packages are also available that will help with all manner of direct marketing administration – eg, address/name de-duplication, postcodes checking and verification, etc. These systems are being improved and upgraded constantly. If a direct mail campaign is to be initiated, it is strongly recommended that expert advice should be sought regarding which package would be best suited to individual requirements.

Telephone call handling

The improvements in the efficiency of our telephone network have enabled the in-bound telemarketing business to boom. This in turn has led to the rapid growth of direct response advertisements. Services are now available that are able to handle thousands of simultaneous telephone calls. Systems are in place that can be tailored to suit individual client requirements, depending on the degree of personal operator intervention that they desire. The digital telephone system gives marketers and customers the flexibility to choose, for example, to speak only to an answerphone to leave their name and address details only or to speak to an operator if further information is required. The decision is communicated by the customer who presses their telephone keypad as instructed.

Computer networking

Now that computers are able to communicate with each other, assuming that the appropriate soft- and hardware is installed, the possibility of solely computer-based marketing communications is now a reality. The Internet has been established for many years as a communication vehicle between academic establishments to enable them to share information. Its viability as a direct marketing communication tool is as yet unproven in the long term, but its potential is undeniable. Already it has millions of subscribers on a worldwide basis. This topic will be discussed in greater detail in Chapter 12.

This is a brief summary of the main technological advances that to date have impacted on direct marketing; no doubt there will be many more in the future.

MEDIA FRAGMENTATION

Since the early 1980s there has been no less than a revolution in the media that have been used historically in marketing communications. Every single one of the main media has been affected by increasing competition, which has resulted in a fragmentation of media usage patterns.

Television

In 1980 only one commercial television station was available. It was in this decade that the pace and pattern of change of this communications channel was set. Within the 1980s, TVAM (now GMTV), Channel 4, night-time, coffee-time and, importantly, satellite and cable television were launched.

The full impact of cable and satellite television has yet to be felt, but already over 20 per cent of UK households have access to these services. By the year 2000, over 60 per cent of the UK will have access to cable television should viewers wish to subscribe. The cable package offers more than access to extra television channels. Its primary sales platform to date has been the related cheap telephone service that it offers, not the extra choice of television channels.

There are currently more than 40 English language-based channels on offer. This figure will continue to increase as new channels are made available. There is the technological capability for about 250 channels to be received by each home which is connected to either cable or satellite.

In multi-channel homes, the research data available suggests that media usage patterns change; satellite or cable forms a substantial part of the viewing time and, within this selection, diverse viewing patterns of the channels which are available occurs.

Table 2.1 *Share of viewing (all homes) Target: housewives*

TV Channel	% Share of viewing
BBC 1	33
BBC2	10
ITV	39
Channel 4	11
GMTV	2
Satellite	5

Source: BARB, January 1995

Table 2.2   *Share of viewing (satellite homes) Target: Housewives*

TV Channel	% Share of viewing
BBC1	25
BBC2	6
ITV	33
Channel 4	7
GMTV	2
Satellite	27
Within satellite viewing pattern:	
Sky One	4.6
Sky Movies	3.4
Movie Channel	3.5
Sky Sport	2.8
Sky Sport 2	0.4
Sky News	1.3
Sky Movies Gold	0.7
MTV	0.6
VH1	0.5
Children's channel	0.4
UK Gold	3.2
Discovery	0.7
Bravo	0.7
Nickleodeon	0.4
Family Channel	0.3
Cartoon Network	1.1
UK Living	0.8
Eurosport	0.9
Others/cable	1.2

Source: BARB, January 1995

The implications of these changes for advertisers are obvious. It will become more and more difficult to predict audience viewing patterns. This in turn could make it more difficult to plan television air-time cost-effectively.

Television media fragmentation may still be in its infancy. As television is the principal medium for many advertisers, it is understandable that they have started to look at direct marketing as a potential tool to help to redress these potential short-comings.

National press

The slow and inexorable decline of newspaper sales continues. Newspapers still remain, however, a very potent and influential communication tool. In an effort to keep their offerings ever more interesting, newspapers have turned to 'supplementation' to bolster their sales. This has obvious attractions for their readers who are offered free extras in their paper, such as sport, television listings, health, women's issues, cookery, etc.

This is a double-edged sword for advertisers. It has obvious attractions as there is the potential to target different audiences – eg, men with sport, women with cookery, etc. Unfortunately, reliable, consistent and accurate research data is often lacking to track how these supplements are used and by whom. Without this data, planning national press advertising accurately becomes more of a gamble.

Women's press

During the mid-1980s there was a European invasion into this market which increased the number and diversity of titles available in this category with the introduction of titles such as *Bella*, *Prima* and *Hello!*. Women increased their repertoire of magazines initially, but the recession of the early 1990s has had an impact on sales.

A new category of magazines was launched to increase further the competition within this sector – the 'shop' titles such as *Sainsbury's: The Magazine*. Many have followed the success of this title.

Thus, an ever-increasing number of titles is available for the advertiser to choose from which makes it a more problematical medium to plan.

Men's press

After several false starts this category seems now to have a foothold. The launch of titles such as *GQ*, *Arena* and *Esquire* have opened up the male magazine market to more sophisticated males. However, new titles such as *Loaded* suggest that the male magazine is able also to reach younger and more downmarket targets. It is an area that is likely to go from strength to strength; assuming that the male magazine habit becomes firmly established and entrenched.

Television listings

Following the deregulation of television listings magazines in the early 1990s, there has been a proliferation of titles. This, allied with the growth of more specialist satellite and cable listing magazines, has resulted in the emergence of an extremely fragmented market to replace the cosy duopoly that previously existed between the *Radio Times* and the *TV Times*.

Independent radio

The radio network continues to go from strength to strength in terms of the number of stations, audiences and advertising revenues that are available. The number of radio stations has increased at the local level because more stations have been made available as a result of new licences being granted or existing stations opting for split frequency transmission. In addition, national independent radio is now available through stations such as Virgin and Classic FM. This ever-increasing choice makes it more difficult to plan and buy radio packages, although regional buying groups have been set up to help to alleviate some of the logistical problems.

Posters

This remains a relatively static medium compared with the other media already discussed. In the recent past, the number of poster sites has remained relatively static. The key dynamics have been the demise of the 16-sheet poster, the decline in the 4-sheet format and an increase in the number of 6-sheet sites. This has manifested itself as a better quality of offering with the advent of shopping centre and illuminated bus shelter sites. As this medium accounts for about 1 per cent of the total advertising expenditure, these changes are not considered to be of major importance in the media fragmentation debate.

Cinema

This continues to be a minor medium and accounts for less than 0.5 per cent of advertising expenditure. Cinema admissions have increased steadily since the mid 1980s. The growth in attendance has been driven by the advent of the new multiplexes which make attending the cinema a more pleasurable experience than the draughty flea-pits of old.

However, the cinema will remain however a prohibitively expensive medium for many advertisers to use due because of the limited nature of the audience – ie, 75 per cent of the audience are under 35. Furthermore, a cinema advertisement with good production values is for many companies totally unaffordable.

In summary, there has never been so much choice for customers, irrespective of the medium they are considering selecting. Similarly, for the advertisers there is no guarantee that they have selected the most cost-effective and efficient media in the communication plan. The pattern of media fragmentation is likely to continue apace – eg, it is unlikely that News International will pull out of satellite communications after the investment that has been made to date in this network. Many companies see the writing on the wall. In an increasingly unpredictable media market, they are uncertain where to turn to seek reassurance that they are not throwing their communication investment down the drain.

This is where direct marketing steps into the frame. Alongside the tumult in the established media market, the promise of a medium that can be reliably targeted at customers and above all is accountable has obvious and very real attractions. Hence, many companies are deciding to invest some or all of their promotional budgets in direct marketing. Some companies are testing the water with a view to learning for the long term, but many have committed themselves publically to direct marketing.

Despite the fragmentation of media usage patterns in recent years, many companies are investing in direct marketing because it is reliable and accountable.

Heinz – At Home

Heinz announced in 1995 that it was changing the way in which its total promotional budget was to be deployed, splitting it between an above-the-line campaign that supported core brand values and below-the-line activity to support individual brands. This below-the-line expenditure has been invested in one of the UK's largest direct marketing campaigns – *At Home*. This magazine is mailed to 4.6 million households, with several different versions being produced to target different groups – eg, mothers with children, the elderly, etc. It is always accompanied by a personalised letter and offers a mix of mainly Heinz-based product news, recipe ideas, etc. In addition, each issue comes with personalised money-off coupons to stimulate purchase. In appearance, *At Home* is undoubtedly from the 'home of Heinz' utilising many of the devices that are associated with its pack and the tonality of its advertising – a truly through-the-line approach. This direct marketing programme is being used in conjunction with other above-the-line media.

The investment by Heinz in their direct marketing campaign is judged to have given the world of direct marketing the credibility that it had long been seeking.

THE GROWTH OF INTEGRATED COMMUNICATIONS

As well as technological and media fragmentation changes, there must be a change in approach at the strategic level in the way that communication packages are constructed. Historically, above-the-line and below-the-line communication techniques were often referred to; techniques which were above-the-line incurred commission and those below it did not. This was and still is a somewhat restrictive way of approaching communication.

Above-the-line techniques came to be regarded as the most effective and 'sexy' in the communication business. Those below-the-line were often disregarded as they were thought to be 'naff' and somehow second rate. At best they would be included in a communication package as an afterthought once the sacrosanct above-the-line media had been allocated.

It is now recognised that many below-the-line techniques are extremely important in a well-balanced communication mix – many are the driving force in some sectors. Where, for example, would the cereal manufacturers be without their on-pack promotions to help to secure sales at the point of purchase?

This artificial separation of above- and below-the-line techniques forced 'thinking in boxes', as it was believed that different elements of the communication mix, both above- and below-the-line, operated completely autonomously. This narrow way of thinking was itself perpetuated by separate agencies or departments which were responsible for different areas of the communication mix. On reflection, this appeared to be an incredibly short-sighted way of approaching communication.

During the mid 1980s it became clear that different communication techniques impacted on each other both negatively and positively – hence the birth of the 'integrated communications plan'. It stated sensibly that the communication tools, whatever they were, should be developed to the same consistent strategy. Without such an approach the consumer is likely to receive conflicting communication messages which could leave them with a very confused perception of what the advertiser stands for. In addition, it is only with such a consistent approach that communication techniques can work together in a synergistic fashion to help the total communication package to become a greater entity than the sum of the individual parts.

Together with the birth of the 'integrated communication plan', not surprisingly, came the 'integrated communications agency'. Advertising, promotions, public relations and direct mail agencies, fearful of missing out on any potential revenue, embarked on a series of mergers and acquisitions to position themselves as total communication specialists.

Those seeking to use an integrated communications mix should not feel that this 'one stop shop' approach is the only one available to them, although there are obvious advantages in this approach. In theory, you *should* receive a balanced and objective opinion on the most cost-efficient and cost-effective deployment of your promotional budget as there is no competition between rival specialist agencies for your limited funds. The specialists would argue, however, that only they have the levels of in-depth knowledge and expertise to make your communications as effective as possible. The decision on which sort of operation to use – one stop or individual specialists – becomes one for individual companies to make on a 'horses for courses' basis and is discussed in more depth in Chapter 4.

Receive a balanced and objective opinion regarding the best use of your promotional budget.

The integrated communications strategy

Once a decision has been made to promote a company, in whatever medium, an integrated communications strategy should be developed. Its aim should be to explain fully *how* you intend to achieve your marketing ambitions through the use of communication tools. These strategies should be regarded as dynamic and evolving; they should not be written about and forgotten. Markets are constantly changing; the strategy should recognise this and be updated and fine tuned regularly.

Different companies have different ways of approaching the development of strategies and use vastly different styles of corporate language. In an effort to strip away the jargon, I believe that it is best to start with a simplistic approach to define what your communication strategy should be. In essence, the detail in an integrated communication strategy distils down to answering the following key questions:

❑ What?
❑ Who?
❑ Why?
❑ Where?
❑ When?
❑ How?
❑ How much?

It is recognised that this is not an entirely original approach and it is one that is *claimed* to be used to a greater or lesser extent by many agencies or companies alike to help to organise their thinking. There is a tendency for many of these organisations to rush this initial planning phase in the desire to get on to the more interesting part of the job – that of developing interesting creative material to bring their strategy to life.

It is not possible to spend too much time or effort in the preparation of this initial communication strategy. Without solid thinking at this first stage it will be unlikely that a successful finalised communication mix will result. This overall strategy encompasses planning for all the potential communication tools. The role that direct marketing will play ultimately within this plan will be determined by the nature of the finalised strategy.

Developing a communication strategy

The starting point for this exercise is desk research to pull together all of the existing information that is available on your product or service. The object of this exercise is to appraise fully the current market situation. Without such base knowledge it will be difficult to determine where the company wishes to be in the future. Within many companies there is often a vast reserve of available data, but it may not all be available at a single source. This may involve a certain degree of detective work to track it down and to assimilate it into a usable format.

Information gaps may still exist after this initial trawling together of data. The gaps in knowledge may be able to be filled by purchasing data or research. Data purchased for such purposes, such as pre-published reports by research companies, government departments, trade organisations, etc, is usually classified as 'secondary'. Because this data is 'off-the-peg', it can be relatively inexpensive to acquire.

If published data is unavailable or unsuitable, original 'primary' research may need to be commissioned. This research can be either quantitative, qualitative or even a combination of both – qual/quant. Quantitative data provides numbers-based solutions and thus gives a perspective of breadth; qualitative research being 'end user/consumer' focused, brings a perspective of depth; qual/quant obviously does both jobs. Commissioning original research can be an expensive option but often it is the only recourse to find solutions to some of the more complex or difficult elements of the communication strategy.

Assuming that all the information is at hand, the next step is to put the strategy together. It is likely that even with a mountain of information at hand, tough decisions may need to be taken to ensure that the strategy is as single-minded and as focused as possible.

Elements of the strategy

Theme/mission statement

This may sound 'corny', but without an overall perspective and approach it is more difficult to pull a coherent strategy together. The theme/

mission statement should set the tone for the strategy. It may be that the theme will emerge as the strategy is developed, as it is only after understanding where the company is at present, where it wants to go and the means by which it is going to get there that a theme/mission statement will become clear.

Understand where your company is going and develop a strategy to take it into the future.

On establishing a theme, the next step is to pull the elements of the strategy together by answering the following questions and then translating them into statements. On completing this stage, all that remains is to rewrite these findings into a finished document, adopting the topic headings/ terminologies with which your company is familiar. If there is no set protocol for communication strategies, those which have been suggested should be retained as they are self-explanatory and will be understood universally.

What?

What is being sold?

At first sight this may appear perfectly obvious and the question may be extremely straightforward to answer. However, there may be more to the product or service than is immediately apparent. You should ensure, therefore, that there is enough background information to answer this question adequately.

What is the overall marketing objective?

It is preferable to have a single objective but, owing to the complexities of many markets, it may be necessary to have more than one objective – eg, primary and a secondary. The objectives commonly referred to can be selected from the following: penetration, trial, loyalty, increasing the rate of purchase, awareness, etc.

What response is desired from customers?

What is the result we desire after customers have seen our communication message – eg, do we want them to be surprised so that they will reappraise us? Do we seek only to reassure them? Or, do we desire an immediate sales effect? The answer is likely to be unique to your company.

What are the priorities of the communication?

It is often the case that many things need to be communicated, so there is a need to prioritise. Try to be as single-minded as possible. If you attempt to convey too much information there is a danger that it will fail as it becomes too long or complicated.

What shouldn't be communicated

For some products and services there are sensitive areas that need to be avoided. Be aware of them if they exist and treat them accordingly.

Who?

Who is the target customer?

As much market information as possible should be assimilated. Unless the potential customer is totally understood, it is unlikely that a viable strategy will emerge or indeed the tools be developed to communicate with them.

The information on the target customer needs to be both quantitative and qualitative to give the depth and breadth of information which is required to locate and communicate with them. To do this, it is likely that many different sources of data will have to be consulted.

Not all of the questions that are proposed are pertinent to all potential targets, but this should give an indication of the depth and breadth of the information which it is desirable to source.

The types of questions that will need to be answered are:

❑ Where do they live/where are their businesses located?
❑ How old are they?
❑ Which socio-demographic group do they belong to?
❑ How much disposable income do they have?
❑ What life-stage are they at?
❑ What is their psychographic/lifestyle profile?
❑ Which media do they use?
❑ What Standard Industrial Classification (SIC) code does their business belong to?
❑ How does your target feel about you – good, bad, indifferent?
❑ How big is the company? How many employees do they have? What is their turnover?

Why?

Why does the message need to be communicated?

What is their current behaviour pattern? Are they unaware of your product or service? Are they aware but not interested? Are they lapsed or loyal customers?

How should customers' behaviour react to change?

What is the effect that the communication messages should achieve? There is a whole spectrum of possibilities; from establishing awareness through to building loyal and committed customers. It should be made clear at the outset what you hope to achieve ultimately. Be realistic, as it often takes time and investment for many changes to occur.

How should customers' perceptions change, currently and in the future?

Change may not always be necessary. It may be desirable to maintain the status quo; alternatively, a total shift in perceptions, or even some point in between the two options, may be desired. This area requires regular appraisal as competitive pressures can often impact greatly by altering customers' perception relative to the competition.

Where?

Where should the communication be seen to be the most effective?

Which tools are thought to be the most effective in achieving the objectives? The choice of tools that potentially can be used is affected by how much budget is available. Quantitative comparison of communication tools can done by looking at their relative 'costs per thousand', or CPT as it is commonly referred to. This is a means of comparing how much it costs to reach 1000 of your target audience across different media/communication channels. In some ways it is a bit of a 'blunt stick' as it gives no indication of the 'quality' of the tool which can affect how successful it is – eg, local press advertisements are a relatively cheap method of communicating in comparison with television advertising, but consider the difference in perception of your product or service of a message which is received through these alternative channels.

Which communication tools have worked in the past?

If a communication programme appears to be successful, it may not be necessary to change it out of all recognition. It is always worthwhile to appraise new methods as they become available and to consider 'testing' them in some capacity to ensure that the communication mix is optimised.

Look at what the competition are doing?

What are they doing? How much are they spending and what appears to be working for them? Is there anything that can be learned from their communications that could be relevant to what is currently being done or proposed to be done in the future? It is often a worthwhile exercise to look outside the immediate competitive environment to see what appears to be working for other companies.

Should any communication options be excluded?

It may be that some communication options are thought to be inconsistent with your desired positioning. This becomes a judgemental choice which can be proved or disproved through research.

When?

What is the most appropriate timing for the communications?

Factors for consideration are as follows:

- ❏ Is there any seasonality in the market – if so, should it be followed or countered?
- ❏ Are there any other promotional activities that have to be accommodated – eg, within the company, within a group of companies, within the competitive framework, special events such as exhibitions, etc?
- ❏ Does a limit on the budget force us into using only 'cheaper' times of the year?

How?

How should communication be made with the target?

What tone of voice should be used? How much information and in what depth do we need to communicate with them? It is crucial to understand what makes the customer 'tick' in order to optimise these elements. It is often only possible to provide answers to this via qualitative research.

How complex is the message?

For communication purposes, the simpler and more focused the message is the better. Prioritise the communication objectives. Make sure that the communication has a 'benefit' at its core and is not just a string of unrelated 'features'.

How much?

One golden rule of marketing states that there is never enough budget to do what you want to do! Methods of allocating budgets vary from company to company. The most popular method is to allocate the same as last year with an allowance for inflation. For launches or special cases, another popular method of allocating budgets is the 'task-related method'. This method states that the desired activity is costed out to achieve the desired marketing objectives and this becomes the defensible budget.

The level of budget available obviously has a major impact in deciding which tools are affordable. From thinking through the communication strategy it should start to become clear which tools would be more feasible than others. It is always wise to plan for a minimum and maximum budget if budgets are not 'guaranteed'.

How does direct marketing fit into the integrated communications strategy?

Assuming that a coherent strategy now exists, it will become clear how direct marketing can play a role. Direct marketing has the potential on its own or in conjunction with other communication tools to help you to fulfil the objectives in all the stages of your integrated strategy.

Let us re-examine the outline strategy headings to demonstrate some of the ways in which direct marketing could be useful. This is by no means a fully comprehensive analysis, but it is indicative of the specific potential of direct marketing.

What?

Assuming that you are now clear on what it is being sold, direct marketing can contribute to fulfilling most marketing objectives and in directing responses – eg, to stimulate trial door-drops of samples have a proven track record. To build loyalty, a mail-out with a sales promotion device such as time-phased coupons is effective. To increase awareness, a direct response advertisement with a freephone number would work well. Whatever the objective, direct marketing has a role in helping these ambitions to be fulfilled.

Using direct marketing is an excellent discipline to force the main communication points or actions to be prioritised. As previously mentioned, the success or failure of the communication can be monitored to verify whether the communication was sufficiently focused.

Who?

Direct marketing has some of the most developed and sophisticated means of isolating and contacting specific target audiences irrespective of their size or complexity. The ability to target without apparent waste is perhaps the most attractive quality of this discipline.

Why?

Direct marketing has the ability to change behaviour and perceptions. Its effects may not be as dramatic or indeed as rapid as those achieved with a heavy above-the-line approach, but if it is used in conjunction with above-the-line advertising, the efficacy of communication can potentially be enhanced – eg, running a television advertisement with a direct response telephone number will capture a data base of potential consumers which could be used for follow-up direct marketing purposes.

For many companies, a heavy above-the-line presence may be unaffordable or impractical – hence, direct marketing provides a vehicle to enable you to communicate with your consumers, to open a dialogue with them and to build a relationship which could change their behaviour and perceptions in the long term.

Where?

Without wishing to be over-repetitive, direct marketing – if it is not already part of your communication mix – should be reappraised immediately for inclusion. Whatever criteria is used to judge its efficacy – ie, CPT, quality, or the competitive framework – direct marketing can be judged to have undeniable merits.

How?

Because it is a diverse set of disciplines, direct marketing provides the opportunity to find and tailor the correct tone of voice and language to communicate with your consumer to optimise the response. Direct marketing is immensely flexible to cope with a vast array of communication problems irrespective of their simplicity or complexity – eg, consider the volume and quality of information that can be conveyed in a 'snapshot' 30-second television advertisement versus a 'feature length', well-written direct mail-shot.

How much?

The size of your budget obviously will determine the size, scope and nature of your finalised communications plan. Direct marketing has great attractions because campaigns can be highly tailored to be as large or as small as affordable. Unlike television advertising, for example, there is not a prohibitive £100,000 production cost entry barrier to produce a commercial.

Direct marketing can be an effective medium even when only a limited budget is available.

Direct marketing should no longer be viewed as a 'marginal' communication tool. Its strengths, if used in isolation or in conjunction with other tools, are undeniable. We are only at the beginning of understanding and exploiting the true potential of this multi-faceted discipline. Planning and preparing an integrated strategy is the starting point to understand how and where direct marketing could be of use in marketing communications.

Chapter 3
The Facts and Figures of Direct Mail

WHAT IS DIRECT MAIL?

Of all the direct marketing tools, direct mail attracts the largest share of expenditure. Research conducted by the Direct Marketing Association Research Centre estimated that in 1995 in excess of £1.1 billion was spent in this sector. Direct mail is defined as personally addressed advertising that is delivered through the post to a home or business address.

The direct mail industry is very clear about the distinction between direct mail, which is addressed, and other forms of communication which fall through the letterbox unaddressed – ie, door-to-door or door-drops. Door-drops are regarded as a different category of communication; they consist mainly of leaflets, sales promotion devices, free newspapers, etc. These can be targeted only at postal sector level rather than by individual and personal address. This topic is covered in more detail in Chapter 10.

GROWTH OF DIRECT MAIL

Over the past ten years, direct mail has had an incredible track record of growth. The volume of direct mail is estimated to have increased by 123 per cent, while expenditure on this medium increased by 155 per cent during the same period. These growth rates have been relatively steady year on year. However, there have been a few exceptional years, such as 1989, when growth was very dramatic, and others, such as 1991, when there was a slight decline.

In summary, it is a very healthy picture that highlights the fact that direct mail has been one of the fastest growing media in the recent past.

The total size and growth rates of the direct mail sector in volume and value terms is outlined in Table 3.1.

Table 3.1   *Direct mail expenditure and volume, 1985–95*

Total volume (million items)		% Change year on year	% Change 1984 vs 1994	Total spend (£ millions)	% Change year on year	% Change 1984 vs 1994
1985	1303	+3		445	37	
1986	1401	8		474	7	
1987	1626	16		483	2	
1988	1766	9		530	10	
1989	2117	20		758	43	
1990	2272	7		930	23	
1991	2122	7		895	4	
1992	2246	6		945	6	
1993	2436	8		904	5	
1994	2730	12		1,050	16	
1995	2908	7	123	1,135	8	155

Source: Royal Mail

The growth in direct mail has occurred in both the consumer and the business-to-business sectors. The average British household now receives 7.3 items of direct mail per month and business managers are sent an average of 15 items per week.

Direct mail is a fast-growing medium in both the consumer and the business-to-business sectors.

WHO SENDS DIRECT MAIL?

Consumer sector

The mail order sector traditionally has been the largest source of direct mail. It still remains one of the major players, but its dominant position has been taken over by the total financial services sector which now makes up the largest category, accounting for over 26 per cent of the volume of direct mail.

Table 3.2 illustrates the detail of the volume of direct mail that is sent by different sections of industry.

The 'others' category, which includes companies in the fields of, for example, entertainment, FMCG and local government, is substantial. Unfortunately, further data is not available to provide more in-depth detail on this sector.

Table 3.2   *Senders of consumer direct mail, 1995*

Industry sector	% of volume
Mail order	18.2
Insurance	10.3
Credit card	4.7
Bank/Girobank	8.2
Building society	2.3
Retailers	8.2
Magazines	2.7
Estate agent	0.5
Manufacturer	7.2
Book club	4.7
Charity	6.8
Gas/Electricity Board	2.5
Film company	0.6
Others	23
Total	**100**

Source: Royal Mail Consumer Panel

Business-to-business sector

Within the business-to-business sector, the Business-to-Business Direct Mail Trends Survey, conducted by the Direct Mail Information Service, gives an indication of the volume and origins of letters sent in this sector. The detail of this Survey is included in Table 3.3

Table 3.3   *Business-to-Business Direct Mail Trends Survey, 1994*

All direct mail received	% of volume
Conferences/courses/seminars	15
Industry specific	11
Telecoms/IT/software	11
Equipment suppliers	9
Business services	9
Publishers	7
Education/training/development	6
Mail order for office equipment/stationery	5
Retailers/shops	3
Advertising/marketing	2
People transport (cabs, airlines)	2
Others*	20

* No other company type accounted for more than 1 per cent of mail received.
Base: 2747 pieces of mail analysed.

Source: Business-to-Business Direct Mail Trends Survey, 1994.

Seminars and conferences had the biggest share of the actual voice. The largest category, 'others', is not broken down in this survey as each category accounted for less than 1 per cent of the mail received.

Comparing trends in consumer and business-to-business mail usage

On comparing the relative volume figures of the two sectors (Figure 3.1), business-to-business direct mail in 1995 accounted for approximately one quarter of all the direct mail sent, indicating that it is currently a less 'active' sector than its consumer counterpart. Historically, this appears always to have been the case.

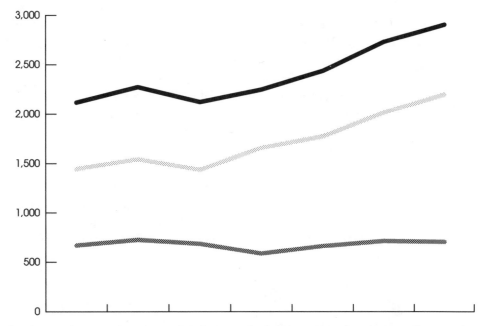

		1989	1990	1991	1992	1993	1994	1995
Total	━━	2,117	2,272	2,122	2,246	2,436	2,730	2,905
Consumer		1,445	1,544	1,435	1,658	1,772	2,015	2,198
Business		672	728	687	588	664	715	707

Figure 3.1   Direct mail volume – millions of items

Source: Royal Mail

Business-to-business direct mail appears to be on a downward trend if comparisons are made with the volume shares of the consumer direct mail sector; figures have fallen from a high of 32 per cent in 1989–91 to 24 per cent in 1995.

The volume growth pattern of business-to-business direct mail has been somewhat erratic; it is slowly but steadily increasing, but to date has not replicated the growth rates of the consumer sector. It is likely that the business-to-business sector has not yet totally accepted direct mail as a 'first choice' communication or promotional tool – hence the apparent lack of firm commitment to it. As this is one sector that is crying out for a 'no waste/precisely targeted' communication medium, this is somewhat surprising. It does indicate, however, the unexploited potential in this business area.

In the future, it is likely that companies which are more marketing literate will be more highly predisposed to use direct mail for business-to-business purposes – assuming, of course, that they are not currently doing so.

It may be that, at present, some companies are currently happy to use direct mail to communicate with consumers but have not yet realised its potential to talk to clients further down their supply chain. Many companies may even be totally unaware of the potential of this medium.

The business-to-business sector in its totality is often characterised by following the trends that were established first in the consumer sector. It is likely that direct business-to-business mail communications are currently poised to grow rapidly, mirroring the growth patterns of consumer direct mail. It has by no means started to fulfil its potential and is judged to be still very much in its infancy as a communication medium.

THE CONSUMER SECTOR

The items that are received through the average consumer letterbox are usually categorised into four distinct groups: personal mail, direct mail, free newspapers and leaflets/coupons. Research that has been published by the Royal Mail Consumer Panel provides information on the receipt of these items by socio-economic group. In summary, this research highlights the following:

❏ The wealthier the household is, the more likely it is to be targeted with direct mail – ie, AB households.

❑ Upmarket and mass-market households, AB C1, have a greater propensity to receive leaflets/coupons.
❑ Mass-market and downmarket households, C1/DE, are targeted more readily with free newspapers.

The detail of this research is detailed in Figure 3.2

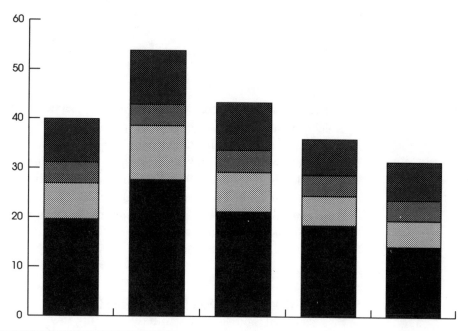

		All households	AB	C1	C2	DE
Personal mail	▬	19.6	27.6	21.2	18.5	14.2
Direct mail	▨	7.3	11.0	8.0	6.0	5.3
Free newspapers	▨	4.3	4.3	4.5	4.2	4.2
Leaflets/coupons	▬	8.7	10.9	9.6	7.3	7.7

Figure 3.2   Average four-weekly household receipt (1995) total items
Source: Royal Mail Consumer Panel.

The receipt of the average 7.3 items of direct mail entering the consumer letterbox over a four-week period is not consistent across socio-economic groups, as Figure 3.2 highlights. However, the receipt of direct mail appears to be more consistent across the sexes. Table 3.4 illustrates that both sexes claimed to have received the same volume of direct mail.

Table 3.4   *Trends in the receipt of direct mail by sex: volume of letters received in a weekly period*

	1991		1993		1995	
	Receipt of direct mail	Share of letterbox %	Receipt of direct mail	Share of letterbox %	Receipt of direct mail	Share of letterbox %
Total	1.6	28	1.7	29	2	33
Men	1.9	32	1.7	28	2.2	32
Women	1.2	24	1.7	30	1.8	32

Source: Direct Mail Information Service.

Data from the Direct Mail Information Service also highlights the older, more affluent age groups; people aged 45–54 and 55–64 are becoming more heavily targeted by users of direct mail. These groups received in 1993 2.5 and 2.6 items per week in comparison with much lower levels of 1.8 and 1.9 in 1991. In the past, receipt of direct mail was more equal across every age group above 25. This is obviously no longer the case and for the 45+ age group, direct mail now represents one-third of their weekly postbag.

WHAT DO CONSUMERS DO WITH DIRECT MAIL?

Research conducted to date indicates that on average at least two-thirds of direct mail will be opened and read. Again, there are discrepancies across socio-economic groups by sex and by age. In general, women remain more likely to open direct mail. However, the levels of opening and reading of direct mail by men has steadily increased over time and they are just as likely to open direct mail and read the contents as women who are more likely to open, but not necessarily to read it.

ABs, who receive more direct mail than any other group, tend to open less of their direct mail, although the proportion actually read has increased over time. There is little variation in behaviour by age, although the 15–24 age group, which receives the least direct mail, is the most likely to read it.

Table 3.5 gives the detail of these trends in behaviour patterns and Table 3.6 gives an up-to-date snap-shot of current behaviour.

Table 3.5 *Trends in opening and reading direct mail (Base: All remembering last item of direct mail)*

	1985 Open %	1985 Read* %	1987 Open %	1987 Read* %	1989 Open %	1989 Read %	1991 Open %	1991 Read %	1993 Open %	1993 Read %	1995 Open %	1995 Read %
Total	83	65	83	66	80	61	80	63	83	68	77	63
AB	81	58	77	53	76	53	83	64	82	66	78	67
C1	86	70	87	62	74	62	85	69	83	67	81	62
C2	82	64	79	66	76	64	77	63	86	65	75	57
DE	83	78	87	74	90	64	77	58	82	74	75	68
Men	79	63	76	59	75	62	75	58	81	69	72	60
Women	87	66	91	73	84	61	85	67	86	68	87	67

* 1989–95 'Read' includes items opened by someone other than the respondent (2–3%), 1985–87 only items that the respondent opened personally are included.

Source: Direct Mail Information Service

Table 3.6 *Treatment of last item of direct mail by socio-economic group, age and sex (Base: last item that was received)*

	Opened & read %	Opened only %	Did not open %
Total	63	14	22
AB	67	22	22
C1	62	19	18
C2	57	18	22
DE	68	7	24
15–24	77	10	12
25–34	63	17	20
35–44	62	2	35
45–54	57	18	24
55–64	58	14	22
65+	64	20	12
Men	60	12	27
Women	67	15	17

Source: Direct Mail Information Service

WHAT DOES THE BUSINESS-TO-BUSINESS SECTOR DO WITH DIRECT MAIL?

From research that has been conducted by the Direct Mail Information Service, many insights have been made into how direct mail is treated by this sector. While it is often possible to target accurately the mail-shot by both name and job title, up to 24 per cent of the target may never receive it as they have their mail intercepted by a 'filterer'. These filterers are typically secretaries, personal assistants or administration support staff and are most likely to be found in larger business organisations, government institutions and the Civil Service. The survey found that 54 per cent of the filterers pass on every item of direct mail to its intended target but, unfortunately, 42 per cent are instructed not to do so. However, filterers can prove useful in redirecting inaccurately targeted mail to more appropriate members of staff within a business.

It was indicated that total wastage levels in this medium are quite impressive, with only 16 per cent of the direct mail received being totally discarded; 27 per cent is kept for future reference or is passed on to a member of staff to whom the mailing may be more relevant. Table 3.7 below gives the detail on how direct mail is treated within the business-to-business context.

Table 3.7   *Treatment of business direct mail*

Treatment of business mail	%
Read then thrown away	54
Redirected	17
Discarded	16
Filed	10
Response	3
Returned to sender	*

* Less than 0.5%

Source: Direct Mail Information Service

ATTITUDES TO DIRECT MAIL

Much research has been conducted by the Direct Mail Information Service into both consumer and business attitudes to direct mail. A summary of the findings is as follows.

Consumer attitudes

Privacy

Direct mail is not necessarily viewed as an intrusion of privacy. It is thought of as being at worst an irritation, but where goods or services were of interest, it was considered to be positively beneficial.

Despite 'opt-out' boxes being included on most mailings, the research indicated that few people take the opportunity to have their names deleted when it is offered to them. Almost two-thirds of consumers who have responded to direct mail have noticed opt-out boxes. People still have a strong belief that permission should be sought before their name is supplied to other companies.

Knowledge of mailing list sources

Consumers are becoming more familiar with the methodology of direct mail: 81 per cent of respondents in recent research were able to name a method by which mailing lists are produced. There is awareness that the electoral register is used, that firms sell mailing lists and that lists are compiled from records of previous transactions. In addition, 72 per cent of the respondents of this research took it for granted that further mail would be received as a result of replying to an advertisement.

Direct mail receipt

In general terms, consumers are happier to receive direct mail from companies that they are currently dealing with or are already familiar with. Correspondence from these companies with whom a dialogue already exists is seen in a far more positive light than mail-shots which were seen to have arrived unsolicited. In fact, consumers view correspondence from companies with whom they have dealings as being totally justifiable.

'Cold mailings' are not as successful as those from companies the consumer is familiar with.

The difficulty for 'cold' mailings is first to succeed in breaking through this initial 'reluctance barrier' to receiving unsolicited mail and secondly to convince the consumer of the worth of the correspondence. If this is accomplished, it will ensure that further communications will be viewed as 'dialogue' and not as further intrusions.

Satisfaction levels on responding to direct mail

Research conducted by the Direct Mail Information Service and illustrated in Figure 3.3 shows the positive shift in satisfaction levels with goods and services that have been purchased via direct mail. Overall satisfaction levels have risen from 76 per cent in 1989 to 88 per cent in 1995.

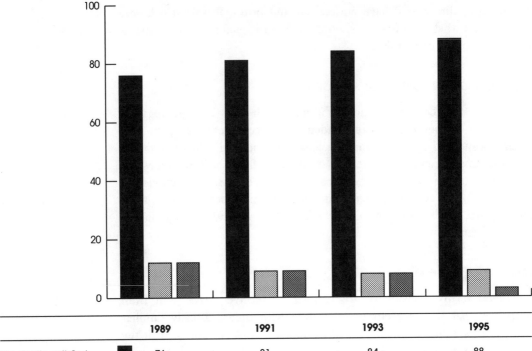

		1989	1991	1993	1995
Very/quite satisfied	■	76	81	84	88
Not very/at all satisfied	▨	12	9	8	9
Don't know	▨	12	9	8	3

Figure 3.3 Satisfaction levels with direct mail purchases

Perceived benefits of buying through the post

Having used direct mail for purchasing goods and services, consumer satisfaction levels with the service offered have increased and any initial dislikes have tended to diminish. Again, once a rapport has been established, the 'selling' task appears to become infinitely more easy.

The most important reason given for using direct mail is 'convenience/ easier than shopping', followed by 'price' and 'not available elsewhere'. Table 3.8 gives the details of this research.

Table 3.8   *Consumer perceived benefits of buying through the post*

Benefit	'Cold contact' * %	Previous contact %
Convenience	22	39
Price	27	35
Not available elsewhere	13	22
Good quality/good buy	11	8
Easy to pay/credit	5	7
No benefits	12	6

* Cold contact indicates that no prior contact with the company that sent the mailing.

Source: Direct Mail Information Service.

Table 3.9   *Business attitudes to direct mail*

		Responsive consumers % *	Direct mail practitioners % **
Dealing direct is a quicker, more efficient way to do business.	All agree	54	68
	All disagree	25	24
You never know when the information you are sent about products or services will be useful.	All agree	62	83
	All disagree	17	15
I like to keep the advertising I receive in the post as a source of information.	All agree	34	56
	All disagree	54	26
I am happy to receive information by post. You can always throw it away if it doesn't interest you.	All agree	81	89
	All disagree	13	8
I feel that advertising mail sent to me (at home) is an intrusion.	All agree	32	50
	All disagree	52	38
I enjoy receiving things in the post.	All agree	64	46
	All disagree	15	43
I really enjoy entering competitions.	All agree	41	18
	All disagree	41	50

*Base: over 400. **Base: 408, unweighted, first stage.

Source: The Users Survey: Direct Mail Information Service.

Business-to-business attitudes

Of those who received business-to-business direct mail, most had a positive attitude to the medium; it was accepted as a necessary and often helpful communication medium. The attitude towards direct mail for the business community is improving all the time. Three years ago, 43 per cent of business managers who were interviewed found direct mail to be either 'very useful' or 'quite useful'; this figure has now increased to 51 per cent.

There is a growing positive response to direct mailing from the business sector.

Compared to consumers, business people who use direct mail for their own marketing are much more positive about receiving it. The scale of this positive response is illustrated in Table 3.9. Business people are less likely to enter competitions, however, and are more hostile to being targeted at home in their professional capacity.

Chapter 4

How to Get a Direct Mail Campaign Started

Once the decision has been made that direct mail should be included in the communication mix, the following issues need to be resolved, irrespective of the fact that a company may be new to direct mail or has already used it in the past.

It is not too complicated to pull a direct mail campaign together. It does call, however for a degree of organisation as more steps and stages are involved than may be the case with planning other elements of the communication mix. Being organised from the start will ensure that nothing is forgotten or left to chance. This chapter will explain all the initial planning procedures that need to be put into place to get campaign development under way.

The decisions and planning procedures that need to be put into place fall into the following four categories:

1. Deciding who will be responsible for initiating the work both internally and/or externally.
2. Putting the planning procedures/logistics into place that will get the campaign off the ground.
3. Following procedures/guidelines on conducting external briefings.
4. Putting into place working practices that will optimise external working relationships.

WHO WILL BE RESPONSIBLE FOR PRODUCING THE WORK?

Before embarking on a direct mail campaign, it must be decided first who will be responsible for initiating and briefing the work internally, and secondly, who will be briefed to produce the work.

Initiating/briefing the work internally

The main decision to be made is whether this will be an extension of the work already conducted by the marketing department or whether a new position needs to be created to concentrate solely on the production of direct mail campaigns. There is no clear cut answer to this and the question decision is likely to be made on a 'horses for courses' basis. There are, however, a number of definite pros and cons of either outcome.

Pros of sole marketing department responsibility

❏ No need to recruit additional staff.
❏ As a single department is in charge of external promotional communication, continuity in approach through-the-line should be ensured.
❏ Avoids 'internal politics' when budgets are allocated as the marketing department has full responsibility for deciding differences – ie, there is no in-fighting.

Cons of sole marketing department responsibility

❏ The department may already be 'stretched' and thus will not have enough time to devote to developing a new communication approach.
❏ As new skills and procedures have to be learned, mistakes are likely to be made and time will be lost during the learning phase.
❏ The department may not be fully committed to the potential of direct mail owing to non-familiarity so it may instinctively give preference to alternative communication tools with which it is already familiar.

Pros of having 'specialist' responsibility

❏ Because the marketing department is solely responsible for direct mail, attention can be focused on producing the best possible campaign.
❏ In-depth knowledge of procedures and logistics will eliminate mistakes and time wasting.
❏ Sole responsibility may be more cost-effective in the long run as it

will ensure that the job is done 'properly' rather than being tagged on to existing responsibilities.

❏ The marketing department is in touch with other 'direct specialists' and thus will be aware of developments, and new products and procedures as they come on stream.

Cons of having 'specialist' responsibility

❏ Extra costs as a new person may have to be employed.
❏ It may be difficult for the department to instil a 'direct culture' if there is internal politics or resistance.
❏ It is unlikely to produce an immediate pay-back, therefore may be difficult to justify role internally in the short/mid-term.

Another option that could be followed is to employ a freelance employee to set up the campaign, perhaps with a view to him or her becoming a full-time employee should the project be successful. In this way all the advantages of having a full-time specialist are gained with few many of the disadvantages.

If a commitment is made to direct mail, this approach will only be a short-term 'fix' and in the longer term it is recommended that a specialist is employed. As two-thirds of the top 3000 advertisers already employ someone with sole responsibility for direct mail, this is indicative of the approach that is deemed necessary to run successful long-term campaigns.

Successful long-term campaigns are usually run by a specialist with sole responsiblity for direct mail.

If a specialist is employed, it is a matter for internal politics and organisation to determine if he or she becomes a wing of the marketing department under its control or is an entirely separate entity. For most companies, the former is the preferred option to ensure that the benefits of integrated communications planning and initiation can be reaped.

Producing the work

After deciding who is to be responsible internally for controlling a direct mail campaign, the next step is to decide who will be responsible for actually producing the work. Three possible routes can be followed:

1. Everything is produced and controlled in-house – ie, a direct marketing department plans and produces all elements of a direct mail campaign.
2. A combination of freelance and in-house expertise – ie, the work will be planned in-house, but specialist areas, such as database management, production of creative work, printing of mail-shots, etc, may be produced by freelance staff.
3. External agencies are used – a specialist direct mail agency will plan

and control the development of all elements of the campaign following a client brief on requirements.

In theory, the degree of direct 'control' that a client has over the work which is developed diminishes through the three options: the first option affords the most control and the third option the least. The absolute level of control will also be determined by the quality of the working relationship, that exists between any outside suppliers – the better the relationship the greater the control the client should have. It is not always such a good thing for the client to have total control over the creative output as this can often stifle innovation. As direct mail is still very much an evolving communication medium, this creativity is the life blood of successful campaigns.

Again, the decision regarding which route to follow is in no way clear-cut, as it is dependent on individual company circumstances. The pros and cons of these approaches are as follows.

Pros of producing and controlling everything in-house

❑ The company can retain total control.
❑ It may be cheaper in the long run as there will be no mark-ups, additional fees or commission.
❑ It may be quicker to produce work as everyone is 'on the spot'.

Cons of producing and controlling everything in-house

❑ It can be very expensive to set up initially as many specialist staff may be needed – for example, a database specialist, creative talent, print/production staff, administration staff, etc.
❑ The department may become 'out of touch' as a result of working on one piece of business only. It may thus become blinkered and miss out on new developments.
❑ Depending on the company culture, the department can run the risk of becoming reactive or systematised rather than proactive and dynamic.
❑ The department can be less flexible and quick to react as the 'service edge' will be lacking.

Pros of producing by a mix of freelance and in-house

❑ If good freelance back up is available, the department can provide expertise without any additional overhead costs.
❑ This flexible approach means that talent is only employed when it is

required. This is useful for smaller companies which are not using direct mail 365 days per year.

❑ In-house involvement keeps a degree of control over the development process as close liaison is possible at all times.

Cons of producing by a mix of freelance and in-house

❑ The best talent may not always be available as it is likely to be in demand.

❑ To secure the desired talent, it may be necessary to pay a retainer which adds to the costs.

❑ As freelancers are not fully accountable there could be inconsistencies in the approach or a lack of continuity if more than one freelancer is involved.

❑ It will be necessary to have very thorough briefing and control procedures to keep freelance and in-house talent working together effectively.

Pros of producing using an agency

❑ The agency is likely to have highly qualified staff who are at the 'leading edge' of developments in the direct mail market.

❑ The agency is likely to take a proactive role in your business.

❑ The continuity of the whole campaign is likely to be maintained, especially if a full service option is selected. The agency can control everything from creative development to database development and maintenance.

❑ The agency will be very quick and flexible to make amendments to work as requested as they are service oriented.

❑ The agency is more likely to produce a successful campaign as it is in the agency's interest to do so, especially if is employed on a 'payment by results' contract.

❑ The agency's knowledge of other direct marketing techniques may be useful to bring additional elements to the campaign – eg, telemarketing.

Cons of producing using an agency

❑ It can be an expensive option, dependent on the degree of agency involvement that is required.

❑ It may not be able to influence totally the staff responsible for the account – hence personality conflicts can arise.

❑ Agency staff are not always available to you 100 per cent of the time as often they have other account responsibilities.

Unless the campaigns are likely to run for 365 days of the year and account for millions of pounds of a promotional budget, it may not be cost-effective to set up an in-house facility, although this is the way that many major users of direct mail operate.

The most usual way of approaching the development of direct mail is to use an agency in the first instance to 'milk' their expertise, thus avoiding any potential pitfalls. This approach has the additional benefit of that agency indirectly trains all those who are involved in the development of direct mail campaigns.

Option two is a stepping-stone which could be criticised as it brings many of the disadvantages of either option one or option three with few of the advantages. It is the option that requires the most internal input and control as there are more variables that potentially could go wrong. However, it can be a viable option assuming that the quality of freelance staff is readily available for employment on an ad hoc basis. It does have its attractions for companies with smaller budgets and ambitions who believe that both options one and three are unaffordable.

PLANNING PROCEDURES TO GET YOUR CAMPAIGN OFF THE GROUND

Once it has been decided that a direct mail campaign should play a role in the communication mix and the logistics of processing the work internally and externally have been resolved, the next step is to put the planning of the campaign into motion. It is important to be clear at the outset of the logistics and the stages involved in planning a direct mail campaign. It is not complicated but, as with the development of many elements of the communication mix, thorough planning at the outset will help to eliminate any potential costly mistakes.

Be clear from the outset to plan your direct mail campaign thoroughly to avoid costly mistakes.

While it may seem a little pedantic to have such a 'process-led' approach, it is vital to do this at the outset to ensure that all eventualities are planned for. The choice of who is responsible for the development process both internally and externally will obviously affect who implements the various stages of the plan.

In outline, the stages in developing a direct mail campaign are as follows:

Set the campaign objectives Try as far as possible to set specific objectives as this will be the only way of determining if the campaign was successful or not – eg, to achieve a 5 per cent response rate that converts into a

2 per cent sales result, to raise £20,000 in charitable donations, to improve awareness and the propensity to purchase scores of the brand by X per cent, etc.

If a company is new to direct mail, this may be difficult as it has no base knowledge or experience to draw on. In this instance it would be advisable to set the minimum acceptable response rate as your target. This may seem rather defeatist, but as this is a learning process it may not be possible to optimise the communication potential in the first mail-shot. Also, the way in which direct marketing works to build long-term relationships should not be forgotten. Immediate payback is not always the most feasible method of account.

Depending on the specific objectives, it may be necessary to commission research before and after the campaign activity to measure the response – eg, for changes in awareness and goodwill, etc. Similarly, if sales are to be the ultimate measuring stick, ensure also that data before and after the campaign will be available.

Set the budget This may be a given figure which is non-negotiable. The budget level will help to determine the nature and scope of your campaign. If a task-related budget is being allocated, the entire planning procedure will have to be conducted before the cost of the campaign is determined. This is sometimes unrealistic and can often result in expensive campaigns. It is therefore advisable to have, at the very least, a notional ballpark figure in mind during the planning process to guide the development process.

Identify your target To reap fully the benefits of direct mail, total clarity is needed to decide who the target is. Include as much detail and information, both qualitative and quantitative, regarding the target. An in-depth profile of the target will help to optimise the eventual database/mailing list. The more detail that can be included at this stage the better your eventual response rate is likely to be.

Decide how to reach the target and set up the database There is no single answer to this question. The list of names and addresses that eventually will become the database can be sourced from many different places. Again, individual circumstances will determine which single or combination of sources can be used. The main ways of accessing a target are via the following sources:

❑ Current customer base.
❑ Past enquirers.
❑ Advertising respondents.
❑ External lists that match the profile of your target.

De-duplicate the names If more than one source has been used, the names should be de-duplicated to eliminate waste and ill-will. Software is readily available to help with this task.

Develop the creative package Often this can be the most time-consuming area of development. At the end of this stage, the appearance and content of the package will be determined.

Research the package Wherever possible, a mock-up of the mailing package should be researched to check that it is communicating as intended. This process will be discussed in more detail in Chapter 11.

Produce the package The nature of the package will determine how complex or lengthy this process will be. It may be that several different suppliers will need to be co-ordinated – eg laser printers, supplier of a 'gimmick', cardboard engineers, etc.

Mail out This will be handled either internally or via a mailing house. Ensure that advantage is taken of mail-sort discounts if this is thought to be appropriate.

Analyse response – Check back to your original objectives and see how well the mail-out has performed.

Add response information back on to the database If it is appropriate include any additional information that has been gathered as a result of the response back on to the database. This information could be vital in building and refining the database and making it more productive in the future. This topic will be covered in more depth in Chapter 6.

GUIDELINES ON HAVING THE WORK PRODUCED

When work is being produced, either internally or externally, the starting-point should always be a thorough written brief that is agreed by all parties. A precise brief is a crucial start to the production of good creative material. Every effort should be made to ensure that the brief and the briefing process stimulate the team which is responsible for producing the finished work. A good brief is clear, to the point and, above all, positive.

A clear, concise and positive written brief is the essential starting point of any campaign.

The elements that should be included in the brief are as follows:

❑ Reasons for the brief.
❑ Current market status.
❑ What the direct mail objectives are.
❑ Target profile.
❑ Product story/information.
❑ Competitive positioning.

❏ Budget (if available).
❏ Timing.
❏ Action standards – ie, research and evaluation if appropriate.
❏ Appendix – to be used for any detailed back-up information.

If you are approaching an agency to produce work for the first time in a competitive pitch, the Direct Marketing Association has issued the following best practice guidelines for management of the pitch:

Direct Marketing Association best practice guidelines for clients who invite Agencies to pitch for business

1. The client should provide a formal written brief, which should include details of the components of the campaign or project, and the budget available for the relevant project or campaign. The brief should explain the preferred method of remuneration for the successful agency.
2. The brief should state clearly what the agency is expected to produce for the pitch, and specifically explain whether proposals should include creative work.
3. The brief should explain whether the agencies involved in the pitch will receive a rejection fee. If a rejection fee is available, it should be agreed in writing in advance of the pitch. The nature and scope of the rejection fee should always be confirmed in writing.
4. A date and time for the pitch should be agreed in writing. There should be reasonable time (to be determined by both parties, but not less than two weeks) between receiving the brief and the pitch. The client should confirm in writing who will be present at the pitch, together with details of their job title and functions.
5. The client should make clear to all the agencies involved in the pitch whether its incumbent agency is being invited to pitch.
6. The client should confirm in writing, with particular reference to the marketing trade press, whether the pitch is to be kept confidential, and in particular, whether the names of the other agencies participating should be released.
7. The client should appoint a main contact within the organisation with whom the agency should consult during the pre-pitch process. The client should be prepared to provide any background information which would enable the agency to develop its proposals.
8. The agency should be expected to sign a confidentiality agreement if sensitive material is released by the client.
9. Following the pitch, the client should inform all parties of the decision by an agreed date. The outcome of the pitch should be confirmed in writing. The client should provide the unsuccessful agencies with some of the background to its decision and return their presentation documents and creative work.
10. The successful agency should receive notification of their appointment in writing. The DMA recommends that this is reinforced with a detailed contract which should be signed by both parties as soon as possible after the decision, and certainly before the agency commences work.
11. Copyright in the creative work produced for the pitch shall remain with the participating agencies, unless otherwise expressly agreed.
12. Any incidence of practices contrary to the letter or spirit of these guidelines may be referred to the DMA which shall conciliate between the two parties.

While these guidelines may look forbidding, they have arisen to protect the best interests of both clients and agencies. If these guidelines are followed, agencies are reassured that they have a real opportunity to win business rather than the opportunity being purely speculative. Similarly, it forces clients to commit themselves in a meaningful way to the development of direct mail campaigns.

OPTIMISING EXTERNAL WORKING RELATIONSHIPS

Assuming that all the previously mentioned guidelines have been followed for briefing an outside supplier or agency, the other areas that can cause a 'relationship breakdown' are in the areas of timing, budgeting/financial control, and attitude to teamwork. Some guidelines to help avoid disputes in these areas are as follows:

Timing

❑ The golden rule is that there is *never* enough time to produce direct mail campaigns, so plan accordingly!

❑ For campaign development, it is best to allow one month to produce the work for initial presentation. Agencies can turn work around much quicker than this if necessary – ie, in an emergency – but they do tend to produce a better quality product if adequate time is allowed for development. Relationships can come under strain if a client continually pushes for work on short deadlines. To avoid continual short deadline crisis management it is essential to plan the campaign development adequately, as outlined previously.

Plan ahead to avoid short deadline crises and be honest about the required timing.

❑ Always try to be honest about timing. Imposing false deadlines can often be counter-productive in the long run, as 'crying wolf' introduces an element of dishonesty into the working relationship. Without basic honesty between the two parties it will be an uphill struggle to establish a viable and productive working relationship.

❑ To avoid last minute crises, insist that the agency provides a detailed timing plan to ensure that it is feasible to produce the desired creative package by the required deadline.

❑ Both agency and client should try to stick to the timing plan. Obviously, there will be times when this is not possible. To ensure that matters do not slip too far, insist that timing plans are updated as frequently as is necessary and ensure that they are circulated to all those parties that will be interested in the information.

Budgeting/financial control

❏ Ensure that a structured system is put into place to cover areas such as estimating, invoicing and payment.

❏ Always keep the agency informed of any likely changes to budgets that may affect them – to be forewarned is to be forearmed!

❏ Include relevant budgets in the initial brief. This guides the creative production/scale of the mail shot and will be more effective and less frustrating for the agency which will not waste time developing work that is unaffordable.

❏ If it is felt necessary, competitive quotes can be requested – some clients include this in their initial contract with the agency. Be aware, however, that the cheapest is not necessarily the best, as production values may be at stake.

❏ Before a company commits itself to expenditure on production, it should insist on a signed estimate. The client should counter-sign it as an indication of approval.

❏ If the estimate is likely to be exceeded the agency should confirm this in writing and it should be agreed between the client and the agency how the additional charges will be financed before the money is committed. It is always advisable to allow for a contingency to be included in initial estimates, especially if there are elements included that are not 100 per cent guaranteed – eg, photographic retouching.

Building teamwork

❏ Ensure that regular communication is maintained with the agency.

❏ Ideally, all communication plans should be developed together. Psychologically, if agencies have been partners in the initial planning process, they will be more willing workers on the creative work as they feel part of all the stages in the development process rather than only coming in at the final hurdle.

❏ Regular status meetings should be held to ensure that everyone is kept in touch with what is going on. Try to avoid having them too regularly so that they become a chore.

❏ Share as much information with the agency as is relevant or feasible. Even discuss problem areas; being slightly removed from the day to day detail of the business, agencies may be able to provide unsolicited solutions.

❏ Above all, treat the agency with respect – they are business partners, not slaves. Good client/agency relationships thrive on mutual trust and respect. With this as a base, the ultimate goal of mutual profitable businesses is more achievable.

Chapter 5
The Direct Mail Creative Package

The decision has now been made to get a direct mail campaign underway; a brief has been prepared and given to whoever it has been decided will be responsible for producing the creative work. What happens next?

TIMING PLANS

In the normal course of events following the briefing, and a discussion on timing and budgets, it is advisable for the agency or persons responsible for producing the creative work to submit a timing plan indicating when they will deliver work. If the exact nature of the creative package has already been determined, a production timetable should be developed also. In many instances, this is not possible until the initial presentation of creative concepts as the nature of the creative package is at this stage an unknown quantity.

CREATIVE BRIEF

The other documentation which should be approved is the creative brief/ strategy that is produced as a result of the initial briefing document. The creative brief is the internal paperwork in an agency/creative depart- ment that interprets the client's brief into a format that is perhaps more focused and may be more 'creative friendly'. In many cases, they will find a core creative proposition around which the creative work should be developed.

Typical headings in a creative brief are as follows:

❑ *Objectives* What is this direct mail campaign aiming to achieve?

❑ *Target audience* Describe the customer in as many ways as is appropriate; demographics, psychographics and geodemographics should all be referred to in order to paint a complete picture.

❑ *Background* What is the competitive situation, what are the current beliefs about the product/service on offer and how is this to change (if at all)?

❑ *Single-minded proposition* This is an expression of the core thought that the customer should take away after reading the mail shot. To be potent, it should have a clear benefit at its heart.

❑ *Support* This is the back-up information and facts that give the right to claim the single-minded proposition.

❑ *Character/tone* Obviously, this should be consistent with other promotional material to ensure that the benefits of integrated communication can be reaped.

❑ *Desired response* What should the customer do as a result of receiving/reading the mail-shot?

❑ *Mandatories* All detail which must be included to satisfy direct mail legislation should be included here in addition to any specific company information – eg, logos, letterhead specification, etc.

❑ *Budget* Guidelines should be given on the total budget and/or ideally the cost per mail-out that is available. Without such information it will be difficult for those responsible for developing the creative work to do this in the most effective way.

There is a large degree of consistency between this creative brief and the brief supplied by the client – as there should be or the finished creative material could bear little resemblance to what the client desires.

PRODUCING THE CREATIVE PACKAGE

The normal overall procedure for producing the creative package following the brief and the internal creative briefing as discussed above is as follows:

❑ Rough layouts and copy are presented by the creative team for approval. Several alternatives may be presented or just one, depending on the working style of the creative team. It is unlikely that this work will be approved immediately and often there are many stages of revisions, especially if it is a detailed or complicated mail-shot.

❑ If research is to be conducted, it should be done at this stage with highly finished layouts and mock-ups of a single or alternative approaches. This will help with decision-making between alternatives, highlight any negatives with the creative approach(es) and give guidelines on optimising the communication.

❑ Production quotes should be finalised and agreed by all parties before the work is committed to production.

❑ The package is now produced by whichever methods have been decided upon and mailed either direct or through a handling house.

❑ Finally, the response rate is monitored and analysed, and any findings are fed back into the database.

❑ If non-standard mailing is used, check with the Post Office to ensure that it does not violate any postal regulations.

ELEMENTS OF A DIRECT MAIL CAMPAIGN

Once timings and the creative brief have been agreed, it falls to the copywriter/art director team who are developing the material to get on with their task of developing the creative package that is judged the most appropriate and cost-effective.

Within the direct mail industry everyone is going through a steep learning curve in refining their direct mail creative packages. There is a recognition that the end consumers of direct mail are becoming increasingly direct mail literate and equally increasingly direct mail cynical: once they have seen one car key direct mail gimmick they have seen them all!

The onus is now on those who produce direct mail to make their packages as stimulating, interesting, relevant and readable as possible in order that they will break through the 'clutter' in the letterbox, be read and acted upon as appropriate.

When selecting the elements of a direct mail campaign, it is important to remember that their theme and content have never been more critical. Typically, the elements that can be selected from are as follows:

❑ *Letter* It is the expected norm that a direct mail-shot should include some direct form of communication in a letter. Without a letter or similar written communication it would be problematical to set up the 'story'. This is probably the single most important element of the package. Guidelines on producing more effective letters will be discussed later in this chapter.

Communicating directly by letter is the single most important element of your direct mailing campaign.

❑ *Envelope* The creative approach will determine how the envelope is used. For some communications it may be appropriate to have an anonymous plain envelope. For others it may be deemed necessary to include a teaser/invitation to open. Or it may even be appropriate to have the sales message liberally plastered all over the envelope. There is no right or wrong way to use an envelope. It depends what is most relevant and affordable for your particular mail-shot. Practitioners of direct mail err on the side of including a message of some description on the envelope, otherwise it is regarded as a 'lost opportunity' to get a sales message across.

❑ *Response mechanism* This is the second most important element of the direct mail campaign. It is advisable to consider including a mechanism of some description in most mail shots. A mechanism will be an absolute necessity if you are selling something. Even if you are not selling directly, a response mechanism helps in the establishment of a dialogue where the customer is given an opportunity to contact you. In such instances incentivised questionnaires are useful. Such questionnaires also have the added benefit of providing additional data to help with database management. The response mechanism should be as simple as possible for the customer to use. Separate pre-printed cards with pre-paid postage have a good track record, especially if the information the customer has to complete is kept to a minimum of, for example, a tick box. Include a pre-addressed envelope with the reply device if it is not free standing. Using a 'freepost' mechanism on any reply envelope will significantly improve the response rate. Using a freephone number as a response mechanism can be considered, provided that sufficient lines will be available to cope with the resultant in-coming calls.

Include a response mechanism with your mail-shot to establish a dialogue with prospective customers.

❑ *Catalogue/brochure* For some companies the sole purpose of sending direct mail is a means of getting their sales literature in front of potential customers. It is still recommended that an accompanying letter should be sent with this literature as it gives a more personal touch to the communication, which is all part of building a dialogue/relationship. The nature of the brochure/catalogue design will be dependent on what is being sold. If a business-to-business communication needs to be held on file, it is safer to stick to a more conventional shape/size based around an A4 format. Unusual shapes can be used but they are always a more expensive option to produce – hence, a judgement must be made as to the balance of impact versus cost efficiency. This is an area that research can give guidance on (see Chapter 11).

❑ *Price list* This may need to be included as a separate item, especially if it is a business in which prices change on a regular basis. Having a separate price list will avoid the necessity of having further expensive production costs to reprint an entire brochure/catalogue.

❏ *Sales promotion item* Many companies use direct mail as part of an integrated communications plan by combining it with a sales promotion technique. Examples of sales promotion devices which can be included that could enhance the appeal of the offer are: free samples, money-off coupons, competitions, scratch cards, free trial offers, etc. For many direct mail propositions, these tools may be inappropriate as they may be viewed as devaluing/cheapening the credibility of the communication. A decision to include or not include these items could be resolved by research. Many FMCG and mail order companies seem to have had a large degree of success through including such a device. Reader's Digest, one of the world's leading proponents of direct mail, uses a competition-based sales promotion as one of its core propositions to encourage subscription in the UK through its 'prize-winning draw' competition. This is promoted in television advertising and followed through with direct mail.

❏ *Novelty/gimmick* To include or not to include a gimmick is usually a subject of much discussion when a mail-shot is being developed. There are occasions when it is entirely appropriate and relevant, and other occasions when its inclusion could severely hinder the potential efficacy of the mail-shot. Some gimmicks potentially could improve the impact of the mail shot. On the negative side, they are an extra cost, may be viewed as unnecessary by the recipient, could obscure the offer and, unless original will be seen as a 'copy-cat' idea. Again, recourse to research can help to resolve the dilemma of whether to include or exclude a gimmick.

❏ *'Stuffers'* These are the miscellaneous pieces of unrelated sales literature from other companies which can be included with a mail shot. The advantage of including them is that it helps to reduce the overall costs, as the other companies are charged for taking part in the mailing. For some companies, this is the only way that they can have any direct mail activity of note. However, it could be argued that these unrelated items can have a severe effect on the impact and credibility of the communication. If including stuffers is absolutely unavoidable, at the very least an option should be tested that is 'stuffer free' to quantify the impact, if any, that they may have on the overall response rate.

It is down to the skill of those who develop the direct mail package to decide which and how many of these items should be included in the mail-shot. On a cautionary note, be wary of including everything from this potential list because unless it is developed around a consistent benefit driven theme, it could run the risk of looking too unwieldy, disjointed and a visual mess – not the most productive way of conducting a direct mail campaign.

There are no firm industry guidelines on the optimum number of items to include in a mail-shot; each should be assessed on its individual merits. Common sense predicts, however, that the greater the number of items in the mail-shot the greater the potential for something to go wrong; annoyance levels could increase and/or the message could be lost entirely.

The Business-to-Business Direct Mail Qualitative Survey has highlighted that business people are wary of tricksy creative work that does not inform them quickly of a mail-shot's purpose – they want the information and they want it fast. This should be borne in mind when creative work is being developed for this sector.

Don't try to fool business people with gimmicky mail-shots. Provide them with the relevant information immediately.

GUIDELINES ON PRODUCING EFFECTIVE LETTERS

This is undoubtedly the most important element of the direct mail package. It is extremely easy to get carried away when producing these letters, which can result in their being a less than effective communication device.

Personal research of companies which send direct mail letters would result in most receiving a solid 'C' grade in a report – 'tries hard but could definitely do better'! The following are some guidelines which will help to develop more effective sales letters:

❑ *Make use of the letterhead and letterfoot* It is worthwhile to take the time and effort to design a letterhead which is different from that used in regular customer correspondence. These regular letterheads and letterfoots tend to contain a wealth of information, much of which will be entirely irrelevant to your customer. This information overload can act as a distraction from the core communication proposition – eg, VAT registration detail, company registration detail, telephone/fax/ telex numbers positioned closely together which makes it difficult to differentiate between them, etc. In essence, the letterhead should be 'cleaned up' to make it as user friendly as possible. If it has been decided to use the letterfoot, it can make a neat additional medium to communicate additional information – eg, if the letter were from a builder, the range of skills available, such as plastering, rewiring,

Design your letterhead or letterfoot to be simple and user friendly, carrying the information that is relevant to potential customers.

plumbing, design and plan submissions handled, could be reinforced in the letterfoot.

❑ *Write at length?* There are two schools of thought on the length that direct mail letters should be. There are those who believe that brevity is the best policy and that everything should be included on one side of A4 paper. There are others who believe that 'carry on writing as long as the letter is selling'. As far as these two very disparate approaches are concerned, common sense would suggest that each individual case should be treated on its own merits. There are undoubtedly many instances when it would be impossible to include all the relevant information in a scant single page – hence there would need to be recourse to a lengthier approach. In addition, many direct mail letters simply ramble on and are extremely repetitive, and undoubtedly would benefit from a little judicious editing.

❑ *Offer a welcoming greeting* This may sound trite, but in those instances where there is no access to individual names (rarely, hopefully, if your database is sound!), or if you are unable to afford a personalised approach, it provides a 'warmer', more approachable introduction. This sort of tonality is crucial in the development of the 'relationship' with your customer. So, rather than open the letter with the traditional 'Dear Sir or Madam' think about the target and the purpose of the mail-out and undoubtedly there will undoubtedly be a better approach – eg, 'Dear Parent', 'Dear Francophile', 'Dear Art Buyer', or even 'Dear Trainspotter'! This approach shows that thought has been given regarding the recipient of the mail-shot and that he or she has a hint of the purpose of the communication.

❑ *Use an involving headline to set up the story* This opening sentence should seek to sum up the essence of the communication. Ideally, it should work rather like a poster to encapsulate the essence of your story and have the added benefit of stimulating interest to draw the customer in to read the letter. If possible, it should include a customer benefit – eg, First Direct in their award-winning mail-shot included the benefit-based headline 'Why First Direct gives you more than you expect from a bank – including £15 right now, just for opening a current account'. Many headlines unfortunately are too long, rambling or lacking in a benefit, which is a sure-fire way of ensuring that the letter heads straight for the litter-bin unread. Do not underestimate the importance of the headline. If it is impossible to provide such a headline, it is probably safer to avoid including one for the sake of it rather than run the risk of having a sub-standard one that will impact negatively on the communication.

❏ *Use sub-headings to sell* Split the messages up into readable paragraphs and give each a sub-heading that sums up the detail. The text will provide further information should the customer choose to read on. In a good direct mail letter, if the customer skim-reads the headline and the sub-headings, they should be able to understand fully the purpose of the letter. Without sub-headings, the text can look more daunting and difficult/time consuming to read. The visual interest that sub-headings provide will increase the chances of the letter being read and acted upon.

❏ *Use an indented paragraph* If there is a core proposition that is crucial to communicate, this should be written as an indented paragraph. It is set apart from the rest of the text – hence it assumes a position of importance and dominance in the eye of the reader. An indented paragraph is begging to be read. Try not to overuse this device or its potential power will be severely diluted. Some direct mail experts believe that each page can take two indented paragraphs; this may be a little excessive and could dilute its efficacy. To maximise the chances of the letter being read and acted upon, it is a safer option to use only one paragraph.

❏ *Underlining and emboldening* These devices draw the eye and give whatever is underlined or emboldened a position of dominance and importance on the page. They are devices that should be used extremely judiciously. There is the temptation to use these devices in a liberal way which first dilutes their power and secondly can make the letter look a visual mess.

❏ *Use colour* The same points apply as for underlining and emboldening: tread carefully and don't overuse this device. In addition, care should be taken when using spot colour is used to ensure that it is both legible and consistent with the tonality of the product/service. Some colours, such as yellow, pastel shades or ones with a specific Pantone reference, can be more problematical to read and/or print.

❏ *Use a PS* Similar to an indented paragraph, a PS begs to be read. It should always be used to provide a further piece of information that may help to 'clinch the deal'. It should never be used to repeat a piece of information that has already been given in the letter – eg, 'remember interest free credit is available on all our suites' would be a correct use of the PS. Although 'Have a merry Christmas' gives warm tonal values, it is a waste of a selling opportunity as it adds nothing to the sales message. If there is nothing relevant to use as a PS, it is probably safer to omit it rather than to include something which is ill-considered and irrelevant.

❑ *Writing style* The style that is used will be determined largely by the product or service that is being communicated. There are, however, five devices that can be included within an overall style that can improve the readability and response. It is not suggested that all of these approaches be used in every letter, but they do give an indication of the techniques that have had proven success.

1. *Add some drama to the opening paragraph.* This may not be appropriate for all direct mail letters but, if feasible, it may prevent the letter from being thrown straight into the bin. Approaches that are commonly used are interesting facts, challenging statements, etc – in fact, anything that will grab the reader's attention

2. *Write in a personal way.* Even business-to-business communications can benefit from personalization including a touch of 'humanity'. The degree of the personalisation which is feasible will be determined by how much information you have about the customer and the stage reached in relationship building.

3. *Let the customer know what is expected of them.* Ensure that this is done as quickly and as clearly as possible. Too often direct mail letters can be very verbose and 'woolly' in their content. They leave the reader in mid-air, uncertain about what the purpose of the letter is and what they need to do. Be clear and up-front about these elements at all times.

4. *Keep the reader 'nodding along'.* If it is possible to find some common ground that can break the ice, use it. For example, slightly provocative statements such as 'Why is it that photocopiers are always so unreliable?' gain the reader's attention, strike a chord and draw them into the letter. If the customer and his needs are understood, it should be possible to include an element of this in a letter.

5. *The letter should have a clear structure.* It should be easy to read and understand in almost an extended glance. If a letter has a good structure, it will have a basic flow of logic that links thoughts through an overall theme. To ensure that this is accomplished, find a theme (ideally benefit based), list the points that need to be included as bullet points, and then find the most appropriate way and order of linking these individual thoughts.

ASSESSING THE CREATIVE PACKAGE

At some pre-agreed time the creative package will be presented for comment and approval. It is often very difficult to give an instant reaction that will do justice to work that may have taken several weeks to develop. In these cases it may be advisable to give the work an 'overnight test' to ensure that it lives up to expectations. It is worthwhile adopting this approach when particularly complex direct mail packages are involved, as there may be simply too much detail to assess on one quick exposure.

Before going to print, assess objectively that the creative package lives up to your expectations.

To help in the objective assessment of creative work, some basic actions and questions that can be asked are as follows:

❏ Leave all preconceptions behind. (Undoubtedly, you will have mentally prepared the work yourself! Try to forget how you would do it and keep an open mind.)
❏ Does the work have a clear benefit-based focus?
❏ Look at the mail shot from the customer's point of view. Think about what they will take out, not what has been put in.
❏ Judge the work that you have just received against the brief and ensure that it has been answered fully.
❏ Concentrate on the basic idea and its potential. Minor executional details can be resolved at a later date.
❏ 'Stand back' from the creative work, give it a chance to breathe and come to life.
❏ Is the creative approach genuinely unique? Is it genuinely distinctive vis-à-vis the competition?
❏ Does the creative work feel right for the personality of the product or service being communicated?

THE PRODUCTION PROCESS

On approving the creative work, perhaps after research (see Chapter 11), the next step is to have it produced ready for mailing.

Before you initiate the production process, be sure that you have checked the following details:

❏ Make a mock-up of the finalised pack using photocopies and check that everything fits into a standard sized envelope.
❏ If this is a high volume mailing comprised of several elements, or or if it contains items that may require folding or special handling, check that all the enclosing can be done by machine. The alternative to using

a machine is hand-enclosing which is a much more expensive operation. If machine enclosing is a necessity, the creative work may have to be amended to accommodate this.

❏ If you are using an in-house mailing list, ensure that all the details on it have been brought up to date.

If you are new to direct mail and related print work, it will seem a thoroughly daunting prospect to move from an agreed layout, mock-ups and typewritten copy to the final product which will drop through somebody's letterbox. As long as a step at a time is taken, potential pitfalls will hopefully be avoided.

The procedure for producing most mail-shots follows a fairly similar pattern. The more complex the mail-shot is in terms of the number and type of elements included, the greater the number of variables to go wrong! Hence, if you are new to direct mail, it is advisable initially to keep the mail-shot as straightforward as possible. If many elements are to be included, planning and control procedures should be put into place.

The production procedures most often used in producing direct mail are as follows.

Artwork production

Once the overall design and the copy has been approved, the artwork is produced. This is the base material from which the printing is done. Major changes in the production of artwork have taken place in the recent past with the advent of computer-based desk-top publishing. The procedures have become quicker and more economic.

The artwork will be made up of the elements that have been approved – eg, copy, illustrations photography etc. Artwork is always produced in a black-and-white format, even if the work will be produced eventually in colour. If the supplier is not using computer-based production methods, it can be expensive to make alterations at this stage because it can involve much time-consuming manual movement of the print elements that make up the artwork.

Artwork may be produced for every element of the mail-shot. After the artwork is approved, this is the format in which it will appear finally. Make sure that all elements have been double-checked and that you have 'legal clearance' ie, you are not contravening any of the codes of practice for advertising, direct mail or sales promotion.

Artwork proofs

A proof is a trial print of the artwork, which is the very last chance you have to change anything if errors have been made inadvertently. It is likely that if you are using colour, amendments will have to be made as it is unlikely that the printer will get the colour balance right the first time. If colour photography is used, be sure to check the colour reproduction against the transparency. This should always be done on a light-box. Too often a transparency is simply held up to daylight which is not a very accurate way of judging the quality of the reproduction. Any corrections to be made should be marked up on the proof. Always insist on seeing a reproof to ensure that the alterations that you have requested have been made.

Printing

Finalised proofs are printed up and despatched on to the next stage of handling.

Lasering

To be a true direct mail campaign, at least one element of the package will have to be personalised in some way. At the very least this is a personalised address label. For more complex direct mail-shots this may involve the production of individual tailor-made letters that relate to the personal characteristics of the customer. Using address labels alone can limit the potential of the direct mail campaign, as it falls short in the long-term endeavours of relationship building.

Personalised letters are becoming increasingly more affordable owing to the advent of laser printing. Laser printing gives the option to change the text of each letter during a print run. The most common use of this is in changing the names and addresses that show through the window on the envelope and the letter openings – eg, 'Dear Mrs Smith'. Depending on the budget that is available, variable phrases can be included that relate to your target's characteristics. If a reply device is used, laser printing can be used for printing, making it easier for your customers to respond and easier for you to record the responses by preventing errors on account of illegible handwriting.

Enclosing and mailing

This is the final stage, when all the printed material is put into the envelopes and then mailed. Unless you are sending out a very small and simple mail-shot, it is recommended that you employ a mailing house which will collate all the elements of the pack and put them in the envelopes and mail them for you.

Mailsort, etc

The Post Office has a range of discounts and services which are available to users of direct mail. These services are changing and expanding – hence, it is recommended that you contact the Post Office direct for the latest information. A contact address and telephone number are included in the Appendix.

HOW MUCH DOES ALL THIS COST?

This is the proverbial 'how long is a piece of string?' type of question. Direct mail-shots can be as cheap or as expensive as desired. It would be inappropriate to quote individual costs for producing direct mail-shots as no sooner would the information have gone to press than it would be out of date. The Response Rate Survey conducted by the Direct Mail Information Service indicates that lower than average response rates occur in cheaply produced mailings. Companies which spend significantly higher sums on their mail-shots – over £1 per item – experience response rates of more than 20 per cent on average (See Table 5.1).

Table 5.1

Cost per item	Response rate
up to 20p	2.7
21–40p	7.6
41–50p	5.6
51–75p	4.3
75p–£1.00	9.8
£1.01–£5.00	20.5
over £5.00	41.1

Source: Direct Mail Information Service

Thus, the cheapest may not always be the best. It may be worth giving consideration to preparing fewer, better quality mail-shots as this lower volume approach may produce ultimately a better overall response rate. Doing a split-run test is the only way to answer this question ultimately. This technique is discussed in further detail in Chapter 11.

It is always sound practice to shop around for competitive quotes when large quantities of material are being produced. There are often surprising variations in costs. As this is an expanding area, there is likely to be increased competition in handling the different stages of production, and unit costs may even come down in the long term.

Chapter 6
Mailing Lists and Database Management

MAILING LISTS

A mailing list is a file of names, addresses and related details of a specific target audience. It is without doubt the most important element of any direct mail campaign. It is absolutely vital that it should be as accurate and up to date as possible. Sending even the most stunning creative work to an inaccurate or wrongly targeted list is tantamount to throwing the entire budget down the drain.

An accurate and up-to-date mailing list is the most important aspect of any direct mail campaign.

There is often a tendency to leave the thinking and planning of the mailing list until the last minute. It is too easy to get side-tracked into first producing the creative work and believing that the mailing list will somehow magically sort itself out. The briefing for developing the mailing list should be done at the same time as the creative briefing.

There are two main sources of mailing lists;

❑ Bought-in external lists.
❑ In-house generated lists.

The absolute minimum time that is recommended for a mailing list to be put together by an external specialist company is ten working days. It is possible for a specialist to turn a list around much quicker than this, but the quality of the end product may leave a lot to be desired. The more time there is to develop a mailing list, the better it is likely to be. If an in-house generated list is to be developed and used, there may be a lead time of up to several months. The time taken to develop it will depend on its complexity and the data sources to be used.

External lists

List types

Thousands of lists are available to reach either a consumer or a business-to-business target. The number available and their claimed sophistication is increasing all the time. The main categories of lists available are:

❑ *Responders* These are individuals who may have made enquiries about or purchased from the category of goods or services communicated by direct mail – eg, they have bought a DIY product in the past, hence it can be viewed as being responsive in this category.
❑ *Circulation* These are lists from the subscribers or recipients of magazines. For certain markets they are an excellent means of reaching a specific target, particularly in the business-to-business sector.
❑ *Compiled* These lists have been compiled by specialist companies. They are usually categorised by geodemographics or lifestyle. These categories will be explained in greater detail later in the chapter.
❑ *Business* The main sources of these lists are from data from Companies House or professional registers – eg, doctors, architects, etc.

Who to contact to find out about mailing lists

Information on all the different types of list is available from either the list owners, list managers or from a list broker. It may seem a little confusing that there are three possible points of contact from whom you can obtain a list. Their roles and interrelationship are as follows:

❑ *List owners* They will generate or have access to a list as a by-product of their core business – eg, magazine subscribers. They hold the copyright of the data available for rental. The owners of the lists are likely to have much in-depth knowledge of their own lists, but will be unlikely to give an objective opinion of its suitability for individual usage. Hence, any user would need to be absolutely certain that the list matched their desired target.
❑ *List managers* These individuals can be likened to sales representatives. They take on the job of selling lists on behalf of their owners. Most managers have exclusivity deals with list owners. They will receive payment from the list owner on a commission based system – the more names they sell, the more money they earn.

❏ *List brokers* The role of brokers is rather like an agency media planner or buyer. They will assess a brief from a client on his mailing target requirements and will source the best list or lists on the client's behalf, either from a list manager or owner. They are more likely to offer impartial advice and will have a wealth of experience of using lists which can be drawn on.

The decision on who the point of contact should be in securing a list will be an individual one depending on the product or service to be communicated and the nature of the target audience.

Datacard

Irrespective of the source of any external mailing list, it should be accompanied by a datacard. This will be available in addition to any general information about the origin of the list. The datacard is similar to an advertising rate card and may contain some or all of the following information:

❏ Source or profile of the list.
❏ Number of names available overall.
❏ Number of names that are available, broken down by key selections.
❏ Type of selections available.
❏ Production formats.
❏ Up-date method and frequency for the list.
❏ Price per name or per thousand names.
❏ Price per selection.
❏ Minimum order quantity or price.
❏ Delivery time.
❏ Address formats, postcoding, mailsort.

Direct Marketing Association Warranty

In addition to a datacard, it is wise to ensure that the list has a Direct Marketing Association Warranty. This ensures that the list has been obtained fairly and complies fully with the Data Protection Act, the British Code of Advertising Practice and the Direct Marketing Association Code of Practice. The Mailing Preference Service in turn now holds a reference of those lists that have a DMA Warranty.

Some list owners ask in return that a user warranty is given by the client using the list, ensuring that they abide by the agreed usage contract

– eg, only mailing once, sending a sample of the mail-shot for approval, etc.

Checking that the list is suitable – what to look out for

When a consumer or a business list is used, there are specific basic points to look for to check that the list will be suitable for a designated purpose.

Consumer lists

❑ *Address* This should comply with the Post Office's Postal Address File and include a postcode. Without a postcode it is not possible to take advantage of discounts available by services such as Mailsort. In addition, a postcode may be necessary to help in profiling the target.

❑ *Name, title and/or sex* This should be a prerequisite for any mailing list. If you intend to offer a personalised opening greeting, check that either the title or sex is given. Without this data you may have to choose a more general opening which is target specific – eg, Dear Dog Lover, etc.

❑ *Mailsort* This is virtually standard on all reputable lists. If it is missing, it is possible to have it included for an additional cost of about £2.50 per thousand.

❑ *Frequency/method of updating* Check when this was last done and what percentage was checked. If it is felt that the list may be lacking in this area, ensure that there will be recompense for any mail that is returned marked 'gone away'.

❑ *Where the names come from* Depending on the source, the likely response could be affected.

❑ *DMA warranty* Ideally, the list should come with this. In addition, check that it has been cleaned against the Mailing Preference Service list of those individuals who have stated that they do not wish to receive unsolicited mail.

Business lists

❑ *Usable address* Business lists can provide either the registered company or the trading address. Check that access is available to the one that is required.

❑ *Named individual or job title* There is a tendency for list compilers to opt for including the job title only on their lists owing to the expense of keeping a list of named individuals up to date. Some marketers believe that this is quite valid, while others have concerns regarding the lack of personalisation which can hinder relationship building. It is possible to collect names via a reply device to enhance non-named lists in the long term.

❏ *Standard Industrial Code* The SIC code is a numerical device for classifying types of industry or service sectors. It can be useful to help with targeting.

❏ *Mailsort* See the information under consumer lists on p. 80. Some business mailings, if they are highly targeted, may be too small to qualify for discounts, hence this may be immaterial.

❏ *Company size detail* Check that the measure(s) available are appropriate to what is being communicated. There is usually a choice between company turnover or number of employees.

❏ *Financials* Potentially a wealth of data is available to help to understand what is making a company 'tick'. Data available often includes growth rates, liquidity, credit worthiness, etc.

❏ *Where names come from/updating* See consumer lists, on p. 80.

In general, business lists tend to be more straightforward and less sophisticated than consumer lists. However, the gap is slowly closing as business lists endeavour to learn from the lead taken in the consumer market. Consumer lists differ in two main ways through the widescale application of lifestyle and geodemographic data as a means of enabling profiling and hence of improving targeting and the ultimate efficacy of the list.

Lifestyle and geodemographics

It is the understanding and development of these two areas of customer information that has helped to justify the increasing investment in direct mail campaigns. Used individually and/or in combination, they provide the depth of data and information about existing or potential customers to give qualitative and quantitative confidence that the right people are being targeted.

Lifestyle

Information is gathered about different target groups – eg, basic demographics, salary, product/service usage, social activities, attitudes, aspirations, etc. Up to 150 different pieces of information can be compiled for each individual. Having such information on, for example, current customers enables common patterns in their lifestyle make-up to be isolated – ie, it helps to understand what makes them 'tick'. This is referred to as profile generation.

This is of obvious value in understanding the customer to optimise all communications and to start to build the relationship. In addition, the profile information can be used as a predictive model to find other potential customers who have characteristics in common with current customers. If you are matching an existing database with a new one, be sure to de-duplicate the data as it is likely that some entries may appear more than once.

This matching of profiles is handled by computers and uses sophisticated statistical models to facilitate this. The principal statistical tool that is used is regression analysis. A simple explanation of regression analysis is that it attaches a numerical value to variables in the data and how they relate to each other. This results in a score-card for individual customers. The closer that a customer's score is, on the variables being tested, the better the fit is – ie, the closer their characteristics and behaviour are likely to be.

It is estimated that within the United Kingdom the owners of these lifestyle databases hold information on around half of all households. Three of the more established operators in this field are Computer Marketing Technologies (CMT), ICD and NDL International.

- ❑ *CMT* Information is gathered through its National Shoppers Survey which is distributed by door-to-door, newspaper/magazine inserts and by mailings. There is an incentive for consumers to fill in the questionnaire as usually they receive money-off coupons.
- ❑ *ICD* This was the first company to launch a database that combined lifestyle information with data from other sources – eg, company directorships, share ownership, etc.
- ❑ *NDL* Information on this database is gathered from the data on guarantee cards that accompany brown and white goods when purchased.

This is a rapidly growing area and it is recommended that the relevant trade press is read to keep abreast of developments.

Geodemographics

All the versions of this type of database are based on the census data. The alternative suppliers apply different criteria in drawing together clusters of people in geographic areas who are likely to have similar behaviour patterns. The use of such data is validated by the adage of 'people like us live next door to people like us'. Many of the data sources link this geographic data with other data to give guidance on the purchasing behaviour and attitudes of different targets.

The four key operators in this sector are: Acorn, Define, Mosaic and Superprofiles.

❑ *Acorn* This survey, which is marketed by CACI, was the first of its kind in the UK. It classifies the census data into 17 broad groups covering 54 socio-economic neighbourhoods. CACI have developed other products from this base data – eg. Investor Acorn or InSite that provides information for marketers in analysing performance of outlets or in helping in the decision to locate to new ones.

❑ *Define* This system involves more data sources than its rivals and uses 30 variables in its profiling. The resultant database clusters households into 50 census and 222 financial groups.

❑ *Mosaic* CCN, who market Mosaic, combine information on housing, financial and retail sources with the census data to result in 52 classifications.

❑ *Superprofiles* CDMS, which is a division of Littlewoods, have built this database with additional data from the electoral role, credit references, etc. This database enables the evaluation of existing or potential customers in considerable detail. It works at three levels: 590 initial clusters from census data have been formed into 160 groups which in turn can be accessed by 40 target markets or 10 lifestyle definitions.

Company details of these list operators are included in the Appendix.

Mailing list formats

Lists are now being delivered in a wider variety of formats than ever before. This is largely due to technological developments. There are three main types of format: paper based, electronic or virtual.

❑ *Paper based* Lists are supplied on pre-printed self-adhesive Cheshire labels, which are normally sent straight to a mailing house or production facility to be attached to the mail-shot. Specialist machinery is needed to perform this task, for which there is usually an additional charge.

❑ *Electronic* Most formats can be produced to be compatible with the relevant hard- and software – eg, floppy disc, tapes, CD-Rom, etc.

❑ *Virtual* This is a relatively new development whereby the information is transferred direct to the computer via a modem. This data goes direct to a mailing house or computer bureau, not direct to a client. Those who handle databases in this format are bound by security contracts with list suppliers to prevent data misuse or appropriation.

Costs of using mailing lists

There are no industrial set rates, although certain norms have arisen over time. Most lists are priced per thousand names. Smaller lists may have a one-off charge for the use of all the names, whilse larger lists can have a minimum charge if only a portion of a larger list is required. Straight-forward consumer files average £90–£120 per thousand, and business files cost between £125 and £150 per thousand. If more complicated analysis or profiling is required, additional costs per thousand are incurred. This information should be included on the datacard. For more complex life-style or geodemographic profiling, it is recommended that you contact the companies direct for up-to-date information.

Usage rights of a mailing list

The majority of lists are made available for a one-time use only. It is possible to negotiate follow-up usage if it is required. In all cases the list owner retains the copyright of the list and is the legal owner of the data. All lists include 'seed names' which are dummy records addressed to the list owner or agent. Thus, any unauthorised usage can be detected which could result in legal action.

Legal controls and the self-regulation of mailing lists

Both legislation and self-regulation exist to protect the rights of individuals who may be included on mailing lists and to ensure that no further mailings are sent when this is requested.

Data Protection Act, 1984

Personal data that is held on computer-based records for commercial/marketing purposes should be registered in most cases with the Data Protection Registrar. Personal data is, broadly speaking, information about living identifiable individuals which is processed automatically – eg, on computers. There are certain limited exemptions from registration under the act. It is recommended that companies which hold computer records should check directly with the Data Protection Registrar to see if they should or should not be registered. For example, it can be a criminal offence to use internally generated computer-based mailing lists that have not been registered under the terms of the Data Protection Act. The act gives new rights to individuals about whom information is recorded on computer. They may find out information about themselves, challenge it if appropriate and claim compensation in certain circumstances.

If you hold computer records of personal data, check registration with the Data Protection Registrar to avoid breaking the law.

Once registered, personal data will need to be obtained and processed in compliance with eight broad Data Protection Principles within the act:

1. It must be obtained and processed fairly and lawfully.
2. It must be held only for the lawful purposes described in the register entry.
3. It must be used only for those purposes and only be disclosed to those people described in the register entry.
4. It must be adequate, relevant and not excessive in relation to the purpose for which they are held.
5. It must be accurate and, where necessary, kept up to date.
6. It must be held no longer than is necessary for the registered purpose.
7. It must be acceptable to the individual concerned who has the right, where appropriate, to have information about him- or herself corrected or erased.
8. It must be surrounded by proper security.

As previously stated, it is recommended that expert advice is sought to ensure that any records which are to be used in mailing lists comply fully with the terms of the act. Similarly, if external lists are being used, it is necessary to ensure that they in turn are registered under the terms of the Data Protection Act. Specific published guidance on Data Protection for those who are involved in direct marketing is available from the Data Protection Registrar's office. The address to write to for further information is included in the Appendix.

Mailing Preference Service

The Mailing Preference Service (MPS) is a non-profit making organisation, established in 1983 to foster good relations between direct mail users and the general public. It is supported by the Data Protection Registrar and it gives consumers the opportunity to limit or increase the amount of postal advertising they receive.

The MPS encourages high ethical standards in direct marketing and helps its members to observe the Data Protection Act. It does this by enabling consumers to be removed from or added to mailing lists. Lists from which consumer names have been removed are referred to MPS cleaned lists. This removal or addition to lists is a free service to members of the public.

It makes sense to ensure that all lists that are used are 'cleaned' against

It is wasteful and counter-productive to mail people who are not interested in receiving postal advertising.

the records held on the MPS consumer file. Mailing to those individual who are clearly not in favour of this approach to communication i obviously extremely wasteful and potentially counter-productive.

The services of the MPS are funded by a levy on mailings through th Mailsort contract. Direct mail users are therefore contributing toward maintaining higher ethical standards and promoting a responsible imag that is essential for the industry as a whole. Sponsors of the MPS are Direct Marketing Association (UK) Limited, Mail Order Traders Associ ation, Mail Users Association, and the Royal Mail. Supporters of th MPS are: the Data Protection Registrar, Office of Fair Trading, Adver tising Standards Authority, Department of Trade and Industry, and th Home Office.

In-house generated lists

The received wisdom in direct marketing is that current customers ar likely to be up to three times more responsive to direct mail than new customers. It is logical that, at some stage in a direct marketing campaign these customers should be put at the heart of a database.

Putting a database together

If a formal database does not exist, there are likely to be several potentia sources of data within any given company from which records can be drawn. Those which are most commonly used are, for example:

❑ Current customer base.
❑ Past enquirers.
❑ Advertising respondents.

Depending on the nature of the company and the business sector in which it operates, data from departments such as accounts or even personnel may be appropriate for inclusion.

The next step in the procedure is to decide who will be responsible for compiling the database, the format in which data will be entered and the software system which will be used. If the database is to be fairly limited in its content, level of sophistication and the way in which it is to be processed, it may be more feasible for this to be handled in-house. To compile a list successfully in-house, it will be necessary to provide all personnel who are involved with basic training on the procedures involved. The basic software to handle these more simple databases are often part of a office software package – eg, Microsoft Access. If software is to be purchased, this can be done relatively inexpensively; price entry points are currently about £100.

A basic database record will hold information on name, job title, address, postcode, etc. The more complex databases can hold records of previous purchasing patterns, demographics, lifestyle, geodemographics, etc.

If the database is likely to be large in size and scope, and especially if it is to be used as a predictive model to find new customers from your existing base, it is recommended that expert help should be sought in putting it together. This expertise can be in the form of an employed or freelance database manager or an outside company which can be employed to set up, run and even manage the database.

The theory of a good, internally generated database is that you are able to include only that data which is relevant and of use to you. A word of caution on the material to be included or excluded from a database is appropriate here. In some markets there may be key dynamics that are of great importance but that may not warrant at first sight inclusion on a database. It is necessary for more in-depth and specialist database management to be conducted to help in the decision regarding which data is to be included or excluded – hence the need for personnel with a track record in establishing effective and workable databases when putting together more complex databases.

If complex data manipulation exercises are to be carried out, it is critical that the basic data entry follows an appropriate procedure to avoid wasting a great deal of time and energy in correcting data entries to put them into a usable format. This is particularly pertinent if it is intended to use the existing database as a predictive model to find new customers who share similar characteristics. If the recording methods are known for the databases with which it is intended to merge, it makes sense to follow similar recording methods. Expert advice at the start of any database building exercise will avoid costly pitfalls.

When compiling a complex database, your basic entry data must follow an appropriate procedure to be efficient.

Do remember that, irrespective of the means by which the database is arrived at, it must still be registered under the terms of the Data Protection Act and be cleaned against records held by the Mailing Preference Service.

DATABASE MANAGEMENT

This area of direct marketing expertise has the potential to warrant a book in its own right. It is appropriate here to explain what it is and how it can be used in theory to improve the quality and potential efficacy of a mailing list. Should more in-depth knowledge be required, it is recommended that you consult one of the many specialist books on this topic.

Three principal areas of expertise fall under the responsibility of data base management: database maintenance, database interpretation and predictive database compilation.

Database maintenance

Assuming that the database has now been put together, in whatever form has been decided, it is tempting to sit back and assume that it will now take care of itself. Unfortunately, this is not the case. The quality of the database is absolutely critical in optimising response rates. To sustain and improve the quality of any database, it is essential that basic maintenance procedures are followed. Just as a car needs a regular service, so the database requires regular maintenance to keep it running at maximum efficiency.

There are four basic procedures that can be used on any database to ensure that the quality of the records is maintained:

1. *Postcodes and PAF* To achieve savings via Mailsort, at least 90 per cent of records must be postcoded. This enables mailings to be sorted into delivery order more easily. The official record of deliverable addresses is the Royal Mail Postcode Address File, or PAF for short. PAF holds 25 million addresses and 1.6 million postcodes. The Royal Mail makes up to 2 million changes to PAF annually. It is vital that databases are kept in line with these changes. Revisions to PAF are published in hard copy monthly, on computer disc quarterly and on CD-Rom annually. Revisions can be obtained from the Royal Mail by taking out a PAF licence.

2. *National Change of Address File (NCOA)* This data is also available from the Royal Mail and uses data from subscribers to the Post Office Redirection Service. There are, however, some limitations with this data – eg, as users may opt out of having their details added to the file and it can only be used for matching new addresses to old, it is not to be used for prospecting new customers. This data is available via licensed computer bureaux who charge on a cost-per-match basis.

3. *Telephone numbers* Telephone numbers, if part of the direct marketing process, also need to be updated regularly. The telephone directory is available on CD-Rom. Larger updating exercises may necessitate the use of additional software or computer bureaux expertise.

4. *Data matching and de-duplication* At some stage in the preparation and maintenance of any database this is an essential procedure. Much

software is now available that prevents the needless waste of multiple mailings. This procedure is particularly important if the database has been drawn from more than a single source. The direct marketing industry generic description for this form of software is 'Soundex', although many suppliers have their own versions of this.

The decision regarding who is responsible for this updating and how often it is done will be determined by the size of the database and its frequency of use. In general, it is often more cost-effective for simple, less frequently used databases to be updated by a bureau. Larger, more complex and frequently used databases are often maintained internally as it is an on-going process – rather like painting the Forth Road Bridge, the task will never be completed! It is recommended that expert advice is sought on the most appropriate method of database maintenance.

Database interpretation

Database interpretation is the process of understanding the effect of key dynamics within your database. It may be that for any given database there is a single or combination of factors that will help to determine who the most effective potential or actual customers are. It is the role of those individuals in database management to isolate these variables.

With the advent of increasingly sophisticated computer hard- and soft-ware, this is not the overwhelmingly complex task that it may at first appear. What is required, beyond the ability to work through the data, is the interpretation at the end of the exercise that can transfer any findings into practical and workable information that can be used to refine the database further.

There are developments almost daily in systems and procedures that help marketers to understand their databases. One of the latest develop-ments in this area is that of neural networks. This technology imitates human thought by spotting patterns in data – hence they are good at spotting trends in customer databases. The trends identified are often a combination of demographics, purchasing behaviour, lifestyles, etc. There are some who remain very sceptical about such developments and believe that traditional methods of database interpretation, such as regression analysis, have a better track record.

Predictive database compilation

This area of expertise combines all the knowledge gleaned to date on customers and uses this as a basis to find new ones. It builds on the

Pareto principle that 20 per cent of customers account for 80 per cent of profits. Building efficient predictive databases determines the key characteristics and dynamics of the 20 per cent and importantly gives you the knowledge base to find more like-minded customers to include on the database with the view that they may become new and equally profitable customers.

The key dynamic characteristics of current customers are first isolated and matched with similar characteristics of individuals on other mailing lists. The result is a new and expanded file of names and addresses. It is possible to 'multi-merge' databases using data from many different sources, provided that the predetermined characteristics are largely compatible across lists. Even if the methods of recording characteristics are not 100 per cent identical, it is still possible to match samples, albeit with reduced levels of accuracy. If such merging is conducted, it is vital that the database maintenance procedure of de-duplication is carried out as it is likely that individuals may be included on more than one mailing list.

Chapter 7

Direct Response Advertising

According to estimates from Direct Marketing Association and Henley Centre, direct response advertising as a total category accounted for approximately £1.8 billion expenditure in 1994. It is more usual to look at these areas individually, but it is only when all the categories of direct response advertising are combined that the scale of expenditure becomes clear; this is the largest category of expenditure within the entire field of direct marketing. These estimated figures for expenditure are for television, press and radio expenditure and are outlined in Table 7.1.

Table 7.1 *Direct response advertising expenditure estimates, 1994*

Media category	Expenditure £ millions
Television	398
Radio	47
National press display	786
Magazines display	616
Regional press display	325
Outdoor/transport	45
Cinema	2

Source: DMA Research Centre, 1996

Media-based direct response advertising is not an entirely new medium. It has been used successfully for many years by those advertisers who have offered a freepost or a limited phone-in facility. It has come to prominence more recently with the advent of television-based direct response advertising. The growth rate of this medium has been fuelled further by the advent of more sophisticated telemarketing which has enabled mass-response handling.

The integration of direct response advertising with a telemarketing

Direct response advertising combined with telemarketing is an effective personal approach for both customers and advertisers.

capability has provided customers with an altogether more appealing response mechanism. It is immediate, easier and often a more personal approach than alternatives. There are also benefits for advertisers as this form of advertising is also a superb method of data capture to be used in database building for use in subsequent direct marketing campaigns.

The growth in television-based direct response advertising has coincided with similar growth patterns in both press and radio-based direct response advertising. This growth has been helped similarly by the advent of more sophisticated telemarketing to enable efficient call handling.

The majority of direct response advertising is now via a telephone link rather than being postage based. The post, however, still remains important for some of the smaller and more regionally based advertisers. As telemarketing becomes more acceptable and affordable, it is likely to take over as the preferred medium of direct response in the near future. Telemarketing is discussed in greater detail in Chapter 8.

Direct response advertising has grown also as a result of the move towards integrated communication strategies. It seeks to link together two key communication tools: advertising and direct marketing. In addition, like the other tools of direct marketing, it is an extremely effective way of gaining a feedback on the efficacy/appeal of a communication message. It is not possible to give absolute advice on the correct way to approach direct response advertising; each case and medium to be used must be examined on its own merits.

At one extreme, some companies treat direct response as an entirely separate communication medium, while others may merely tag a response mechanism on to an existing image-based communication. Both approaches theoretically have the potential to work.

In an ideal world it would be preferable to keep the communication approach consistent 'through the line' and seek ways of integrating a response mechanism into the overall creative approach. It is acknowledged that this is sometimes problematic and can run the risk of communicating neither the image nor the response mechanism. It is a challenge for those involved with developing direct response advertising to make the creative vehicles as successful as possible to generate responses while not compromising the other elements of brand value communication. Some advertisers are already successfully managing this 'dual' communication task, Apple Tango being a case in point.

The Apple Tango campaign began with direct response television that invited viewers to telephone if they were having problems with the seductive properties of Apple Tango. The 1995 Direct Marketing Awards record that this award-winning integrated campaign logged 1.3 million calls and helped to increase Apple Tango's market share by 65 per cent.

This is just one small example of the potential of this form of communication. Case studies will be discussed for television, press and radio, which will underline the potential of this form of direct marketing.

DIRECT RESPONSE TELEVISION ADVERTISING

This area of communication is still relatively new and novel in the UK, but familiarity and acceptance of it is likely to increase in the future. There are some businesses that have been able to grow and trade profitably by relying on direct response television as their primary communication medium; Direct Line Insurance is a good example of such a company.

There is likely to be further impetus for growth in this sector owing to the advent of dedicated direct selling television channels on satellite and cable television. QVC and Quantum are examples of such channels and broadcasters. Quantum, for example, claims to reach 235 million homes in 60 countries in all 5 continents and has sales of $10 billion. Sales networks and figures of this magnitude highlight the potential of this area of direct marketing.

The potential of direct advertising on satellite television is enormous, with millions of homes being targeted worldwide.

To date, the most authoritative data which looks at direct response television advertising is some joint research conducted by Channel 4 and British Telecommunications in 1993 and 1995. The latest research was a multi-stage study, both quantitative and qualitative, which was conducted from January to March 1995. The research indicated that this area of advertising almost trebled in revenue terms from 1993 to 1995 and that in 1995, 19 per cent of all commercials aired during the period of research carried a telephone number.

Other estimates of television commercials carrying a response mechanism are even higher – eg, Laser (a media buying group representing London Weekend Television, Yorkshire, and Tyne Tees television stations) estimated that 22.6 per cent of commercials carried a response mechanism in 1994.

Direct response television advertising is of obvious importance to television companies as a source of revenue. Likewise, it is now becoming widely accepted by customers. For many categories of products and services it offers a tangible and interactive adjunct/benefit to an otherwise potentially 'bland' communication message.

Factors that contribute to a successful direct response television campaign

The Channel 4/BT research has been highly illuminating in indicating some of the factors that seem to contribute to more effective direct response television campaigns. A summary of these findings is as follows:

❑ Daytime advertising – ie, 9.00–16.00 were the most cost-efficient times of the day to advertise in terms of the response generated. The 12.00–14.00 slot was the most cost-efficient daypart of all.

❑ The least cost-efficient daypart in which to advertise in terms of responses generated was 22.00–24.00.

❑ The most efficient response-generating programme types were films, current affairs and light entertainment.

❑ The least efficient response-generating programme types were news, religious programmes and documentaries.

❑ On Channel 4 and satellite stations, positioning the advertisement at the end break between programmes was more efficient, while on ITV the centre break positioning was marginally more efficient.

❑ Overall it was concluded that it was more efficient to be the last advertisement in the break rather than the first or in the centre.

❑ Advertisements that had been transmitted earlier in the same day were more efficient than either advertisements that had been transmitted the previous day or were entirely new.

❑ In general, the longer the time length the greater the response generated by the advertisement; 90-second advertisements were found to be almost seven times more efficient than 10-second advertisements. When taking the cost factor into consideration, the longer length commercials – say, 60 seconds – are the most efficient.

❑ Including a voice-over on the commercial significantly improved the response rate by three times.

❑ Keeping the telephone number on the screen for more than 11 seconds likewise increased the response rate by three times.

❑ Including a telephone number that covered 6–10 per cent of the screen optimised the response rate. If the number was any bigger or smaller, the response rate declined.

❑ Freefone, 0800, appeared to be more effective than Lo-call, 0345, in generating calls.

Hoseasons Holidays case history

Hoseasons Holidays are a good example of an advertiser who believes in the efficacy of direct response television advertising. They have been using it, in fact, for 20 years. They use a combination of creative work developed by an advertising agency and their own telemarketing facility.

As a result of past experience and customer research, Hoseasons have refined both their creative approach and targeting strategy. They select advertising slots on the basis of when their housewives with children target audience are more likely to be watching television. These tend to be early peak, breakfast and afternoon slots. Similarly, they have a regional campaign that plays to their areas of strengths.

Hoseasons have found that a straightforward creative approach linked with an 0800 number optimises their response. Similarly, a humorous approach appeals to their customers.

As television advertising is an expensive medium, the budget is stretched by integrating the campaign with direct response advertising in the press to reinforce the message on television. The campaigns have been consistently successful and their success has resulted in recognition by industry which has awarded them the BT/Marketing telemarketing award.

The dynamism already established in this relatively new form of direct marketing is likely to continue. It is not possible to predict absolutely what these growth rates are likely to be. However, if we look to the USA, whose media trends we seem to follow, direct response television advertising is currently estimated to be about 40 per cent of all advertising. It is likely that within the UK a similar pattern could occur.

The challenge remains for the organisations which are developing these direct response television advertisements to ensure that they do not become indistinguishable, 'boring' sales lead generators. They should develop and grow from established creative strategies and continue the job of brand building, albeit in a different guise.

DIRECT RESPONSE PRESS ADVERTISING

The use of published media as a means of generating a response has been in use for many years. For many companies – eg, specialist mail order – it has been their main source of business. Despite this apparent 'maturity', it is judged that there is still potential in this market for growth to continue. It is not inconceivable that in future all press advertising will feature a response mechanism of some description.

Research conducted by BMRB and Mintel indicates that there are high levels of awareness and related response levels of direct response advertising (see Table 7.2).

Table 7.2   *Awareness and response to direct response press advertising*

Business category	% Awareness	% Response
General mail order	76	18
Clothing	49	9
Charities	47	7
Public utilities	46	3
DIY products	45	3
Cosmetics	41	3
Gardening	38	5
Furniture	36	2
Large electrical	29	2
Small electrical	26	1
Drinks	18	1

Source: BMRB/Mintel, 1993

It is not surprising that there are such high levels of awareness as this is one of the longest established areas of direct marketing. Direct response advertising in the press is prevalent across all media, be it national newspapers, women's press, specialist press, etc. A cursory glance through a range of the daily newspaper confirms the importance of this form of direct marketing. The proportion of newspapers carrying advertisements with a response mechanism, rather than being solely image based, appears to be anything from 30 to 75 per cent, depending on the title. An average figure for the proportion of advertising expenditure that carries a response mechanism in newspapers is estimated to be in excess of 50 per cent of the total expenditure. Direct response press advertising is hence already a substantial area of direct marketing.

Press advertising frequently carries response mechanisms that appeal to both the mass-market and specialist markets.

Whisky Connoisseur case history

Direct response press advertising has obvious attractions for mass-market products, but similarly it has a role to play for more specialist markets as the following case history demonstrates.

Scottish Gourmet is an established direct supplier of quality Scottish produce – eg, salmon, venison, haggis, sausages, conserves, etc. They noticed a trend from their database that people were prepared to spend huge sums of money on cask-strength malt whisky – the purest and strongest form of whisky. Cask-strength whisky can be up to 65 per cent alcohol in comparison with a normal watered-down strength of 40 per cent. No two casks of this whisky are the same and they are not available for sale through the usual outlets. Hence, this was a truly unique offering.

The company decided to launch a new club concept, the Whisky Connoisseur, to target these and similar like-minded individuals. These individuals were to be targeted through a direct response advertising campaign, inserts and follow-up direct mail. The objectives of the advertising campaign were to launch their new mail order club and to generate membership.

The press advertising was targeted at drinkers who appreciated quality – ie, they were not the everyday proprietary brand drinker. The long copy advertisements were eloquently written and told the stories of individual whiskies. The advertisements were positioned in male-oriented publications such as the *Financial Times, The Field, The Daily Telegraph, The Times, The Decanter* and *The Oldie*.

Arthur Bell, chairman of Scottish Gourmet, judges that the campaign has been extremely successful. The club now boasts a membership of 8,000 and it continues to grow steadily with annual orders well in excess of £250,000.

It should be noted that in addition to the protection afforded by the Advertising Standards Authority, customers who order goods from either newspapers or magazines have additional protection and guarantees from the Mail Order Protection Scheme and the Periodical Publishers Association. Both bodies ensure that the contractual obligations of the advertiser are upheld and that refunds can be obtained should goods fail to arrive or the company goes into liquidation.

DIRECT RESPONSE RADIO ADVERTISING

This is in some ways probably the most challenging of the media-based direct response advertising techniques to develop. It is estimated that 32 per cent of all advertising on commercial radio carries a direct response device. The Henley Centre estimates that on average 5 per cent of consumers bought a product as a result of a direct response radio advertisement. There are higher response rates for younger, more upmarket and London-based groups, which is consistent with radio's strength among these targets.

As radio is often referred to as 'audio wallpaper', it is the most extreme of creative challenges to develop an effective direct response radio advertisement that succeeds in communicating the response mechanism, usually a telephone number, without causing extreme annoyance as a result of the likely repetitiveness that is usually necessary to ensure that the response mechanism is communicated.

The radio advertising industry is aware that there is room for improvement in the quality of all radio advertising, hence the development of a separate creative awards scheme to recognise outstanding creative work. Direct response radio advertising arguably as a part of all radio advertising has the potential for improvement.

It is more difficult for radio to match the response rates achieved in the press or on television as it is a less intrusive medium with a far more limited reach. The flexibility, affordability and targeting potential of this medium are, however, some of its greatest benefits. For some advertisers the benefits of radio outweigh its disadvantages. There is still much potential for further growth in this area of direct marketing.

Although radio advertising has a limited audience, it has flexibility, affordability and targeting potential in its favour.

Blood donors case history

Radio advertising campaigns were developed with the objective of attracting more blood donors within the London area. The theme of the advertising was 'Give blood – not excuses' and the commercials encouraged telephone response through Teledata. A campaign of 160, 45-second spots ran over an eight-week period on Capital Radio during February–March 1994. The campaign achieved 69 per cent average coverage of the target audience of all adults aged 18–24 years. The results were dramatic. The average number of responses without radio advertising was 79, but when the advertising was on air this rose to an average of 1041. Research conducted among donors highlighted the efficacy of the Capital Radio campaign:

❑ 35 per cent of all donors specifically mentioned Capital Radio.
❑ 55 per cent of new donors specifically mentioned Capital Radio.
❑ 60 per cent of 18–24-year-old donors specifically mentioned Capital Radio.

These campaign results highlight the potential of direct response advertising not only to build awareness but more importantly to encourage direct response in the act of giving blood.

Radio advertising continues to be used to recruit blood donors as it is judged to be the most effective medium at generating the instantaneous response that is necessary to maintain blood supplies in the capital.

In some respects the three forms of advertising/direct marketing – television, press and radio – are still developing and are still viewed as being somewhat novel. The 'crunch' will come for direct marketing in the future when this form of advertising becomes viewed as the 'norm'. When this day arrives, the challenge will be for those working in direct marketing to ensure that response mechanisms do not become invisible. The way in which these forms of advertising are currently approached may need to be reviewed in time. Such reviewing will ensure that the response mechanisms will continue to break through advertising clutter and customer indifference barriers, and importantly will keep bringing in effective levels of response.

Chapter 8

Telemarketing

Telemarketing is undoubtedly booming. Growth in the recent past has been very dramatic. A survey conducted by the Direct Marketing Association estimated that expenditure in telemarketing was £1.175 billion in 1995. Analysts predict that growth rates in the area of direct marketing will continue and that it is likely to be worth £2 billion by the end of the decade. With expenditure of this magnitude it is obviously an extremely important area of direct marketing.

Telemarketing is usually classified into two distinct disciplines – outbound and inbound. Inbound telemarketing is when customers take the initiative to call into a contact number. In outbound telemarketing the call direction is reversed and the customer becomes the recipient of the call.

Several reasons are cited for the dramatic growth in telemarketing in the UK, the principal rationales being the advent of direct response advertising, customer care lines and the growth in the UK as a base for European or worldwide telemarketing campaigns.

It is extremely difficult to estimate accurately what the relative value of inbound and outbound telemarketing is likely to be. *Marketing* magazine conducted research among leading telemarketing bureaux in 1995 to estimate the relative market values of these disciplines. This research indicated that inbound telemarketing accounted for four times as much expenditure than was accounted for in outbound telemarketing. This research can only be taken as a guideline of the relative expenditures but it is indicative of the relative rankings of these two disciplines.

The first decision that any manufacturer or service provider is faced with when deciding to include either inbound or outbound telemarketing in the communication mix is whether it should be developed as an in-house resource or whether it should be out-sourced to a specialist bureau. There can never be a single answer to this dilemma. Each case should be considered on its individual merits. As with many areas of the communication mix, telemarketing is a very specialised discipline. It differs from some elements of the communication mix as, in addition to highly trained staff, it also requires substantial capital investment to provide the hardware to enable either inbound or outbound telemarketing to take place.

If it has been decided that telemarketing is *the* sacrosanct element of the communication mix and that it is the only tool which has proven success in driving the business, it is worth considering an in-house invest- ment. If, however, it is a new addition to the communication armoury, if it is only to be used infrequently or is an additional rather than a prime communication tool, it may be more prudent to use an experienced telemarketing bureau. This option enables the technique to be trailed without incurring an unnecessary overhead burden.

Give careful consideration to your choice between inbound or outbound telemarketing.

The use and guideline costs of using specialist telemarketing bureaux will be discussed in each of the sections on inbound and outbound telemarketing.

INBOUND TELEMARKETING

The prime proponent for growth in this area has been the advent of direct response advertising in general and direct response television advertising in particular. This topic is discussed in greater depth in Chapter 7. The growth of customer care lines has similarly had a major impact in fuel- ling growth.

The rationale for this growth to happen now has been driven largely by technology. The telephone system has developed to allow different tariffs to be made available to stimulate call making, the freephone and local-charge rates being prime examples of this. In conjunction with this call handling, systems have developed that have enabled a wide range of services to be made available that provide an economic means of handling large numbers of calls.

The inbound telemarketing service has been distinguished historically by offering two different levels of service: operator based and fully auto- mated. These are self-explanatory definitions; the former has a 'live' voice to respond to and the latter provides a pre-recorded message and a limited facility for data collection. There is also now a mid-range of service provision that enables operator intervention with the automated system should the caller require further information. This switch between systems is facilitated by the caller pressing an appropriate button on the keypad of their telephone. This facility relies on callers having touch-tone telephones which are not yet in full distribution – hence this is not a service that is available to all. This mixed facility is likely to be an area of growth in the future.

The decision to choose either an operator-based, automated or a mixed system depends entirely on the role it has been decided that inbound telemarketing should fulfil and importantly how much budget is available. Operator-based systems are more expensive but have the advantage of being perceptually more 'user friendly' – an important factor to consider in the process of relationship building. Such symptoms are also more flexible to handle in-depth enquiries if necessary. Automated systems are cheaper to operate and are ideally suited to handle more straightforward services – eg, brochure requests. Customers are becoming more used to talking to a machine, although there are some who remain uncomfortable to use this service and hence could be lost.

For companies who are new to telemarketing, it is notoriously difficult to predict the many key elements of the campaign – eg, the number of inbound calls that may be generated, the rate at which they are likely to come in, when the calls would be most likely to peak, how long the calls are likely to last, how much administration time is needed and what the likely conversion rate will be. If any of these variables are miscalculated, there can be severe financial implications. Experienced telemarketing bureaux should be able to give guidance on the likely answers to these variables from historical data on similar campaigns that have already been run. It is recommended that in addition to this information, more concrete predictive techniques should be used in the form of a pre-test which will help to provide answers to these many variables and to gauge the real impact of a telemarketing campaign.

Use a bureau or an in-house facility?

The decision on which of these options is selected is usually economic, but it is also dependent on the campaign objectives. Outline industry cost estimates for these services to be put into operation are given below. (Please note that these figures should be used as a guideline only. It is recommended that you check with specialist suppliers as they are changing rapidly as this area becomes increasingly competitive.)

Bureau

❏ Operator: £28–£35 per hour.
❏ Set-up fee: £750–£1,250.
❏ Training/briefing: from £500 per day.

In-house

❏ Operator salary, including benefits and overheads: £18,000 per annum.
❏ Work-station with appropriate telephone, headset and computer: £6,000 each.
❏ Automatic call-handling system: from £100,000.

These are ballpark costs only and, depending on the nature of the campaign, further costs may be incurred – eg, to transcribe data, to send out brochures, etc. These figures highlight that the cost of setting up an in-house facility can be substantial. It should be proven, therefore, that there will be a worthwhile return on investment to justify such levels of expenditure.

In most instances the first recourse is to use a telemarketing bureau. It is vital that if you do use a bureau, they are briefed thoroughly to avoid any expensive misunderstandings. It is recommended that the following areas are included in a basic brief. Additional information may need to be included, depending on individual campaign objectives.

Guideline information for a telemarketing brief

❏ Campaign objectives: the bureau should understand fully what you are hoping to achieve.
❏ Describe the target audience.
❏ What is the role of the bureau? – ie, Are they taking orders, collecting information for a database, or acting as an intermediary to collect information to be passed on to a fulfilment house? etc.
❏ What response system is required? Should it be operator based, automated or a mix of both?
❏ Provide estimates, if possible, on likely response rates. (This may not be possible if the company is new to telemarketing.)
❏ Provide estimates of the preferred length of the call duration. (If the company is new to telemarketing, seek the guidance of the bureau for the recommended length of calls.)
❏ State what the tariff rate is going to be. (Research suggests that using a freephone number produces the highest response rates. The tariff selected will be determined by the budget available.)
❏ State the success criteria. It is useful to inform the agency what the criteria for judging the success of a campaign will be prior to the campaign being initiated. Both parties should be in agreement about what the criteria will be.
❏ Test the procedures. Decide if this is necessary and if it is to take place how it will be handled.
❏ Obtain feedback. Guidelines should be given on the desired feedback on campaign progress; is information required daily, weekly or even monthly?
❏ State the lead times. Agree how much notice is required for the campaign start date. One month to six weeks is usually ample.

The cost of using a bureau relates directly to the number of successful calls it answers. What is out of the control of the client is the number of calls which go unanswered and are ultimately 'lost'. Telemarketing bureaux usually give some form of guarantee on what the quality standard for this will be. Obviously, it would be unrealistic for a bureau to guarantee 100 per cent as it can be notoriously difficult to gauge accurately the call flow rates. Ideally, the bureau should have a menu of options available to maximise the chance of the call being captured. For example, all calls should be answered in three rings; if all operators are busy, a queue system could be put into place and/or a facility for leaving a telephone number to allow the customer to be called back when the lines are less busy.

For all inbound telemarketing campaigns it has to be acknowledged that, irrespective of the sophistication of the call-handling facility, inevitably there will be some 'lost calls'. Research conducted by BT and Channel 4 indicated that for the direct response television campaign that they monitored, an average of 22 per cent of all calls were lost. Direct Marketing Solutions have also researched this area and for the sample period that they examined, the rate of lost calls was 21 per cent. This rate of lost calls is significant and highlights one of the potential negatives of inbound telemarketing and direct response television advertising in particular. In order to minimise the number of lost calls, it is essential that the telemarketing bureau are always kept informed of the media schedule and, importantly, of any last-minute changes which are made. This is more likely to be an issue with television-based direct response advertising as spots can be moved at short notice.

Response rates are less erratic in press and radio-based direct response advertising. The former is used in a less immediate way, resulting in a more even flow of calls. Not everyone buying a newspaper will read and respond to an advertisement at exactly the same time, as happens in television direct response advertising. The audiences for the majority of radio advertisements are usually smaller than those for television and the way in which radio advertising seems to work means that the advertisement may need to be heard several times before it is acted upon. It is a less immediate medium than television.

Telemarketing has many advantages, its immediacy in particular giving virtually instant feedback on how effective the message is. It is not, however, a perfect tool as it will never be possible to predict reliably what the response rates are likely to be. Only through thorough briefing and prudent testing will the potential efficacy of the campaign be maximised.

OUTBOUND TELEMARKETING

Of all the direct marketing techniques available, this is the one tool which is most likely to incur spontaneous derision from potential customers. It is claimed by many potential customers to be overly intrusive and too direct in its approach. When people are asked for examples of companies using this form of telemarketing, there is likely to be a spontaneous recall of double-glazing and fitted-kitchen suppliers. However, this is only part of the story. Outbound telemarketing has a valid role to play within the direct marketing mix. Its main strengths lie in the business-to-business field and in continuing a dialogue with existing customers.

The traditional areas of direct sell on the telephone will no doubt continue for those companies who believe that it is an effective tool, but this is unlikely to be the main area of growth in the future for telemarketing in its totality. The growth of outbound telemarketing is likely to be limited because of the creative limitations of this form of communication to sell products 'cold'.

Outbound telemarketing does have some strengths as it can be highly targeted, is relatively quick to use and the response is virtually instantaneous to monitor. On the negative side, it can be an extremely costly tool; some experts rank its expense as being on a par with those of television production! In addition, it is one tool which is totally reliant on the quality of the operators who are making the calls. If telemarketing is handled in-house, it relies on careful recruitment, ongoing training and thorough briefing. If an agency is used, the same criteria apply. In the process of recruiting an outbound bureau, a visit to the premises to hear a campaign in operation is a useful method of assessing the quality of the recruitment and the training of staff.

Use a bureau or in-house facility?

As for inbound telemarketing, this question is notoriously difficult to answer absolutely. If a company is new to this form of telemarketing, it is more prudent to use a bureau until it has proven its worth. If it is demonstrable that outbound telemarketing works, then it becomes more feasible to take on the expense of recruiting and training an in-house resource.

The costs for using outbound telemarketing are broadly similar to those already discussed for inbound telemarketing. One additional form of costing which is used by some telemarketing bureaux is to charge on a cost-per-call basis; this can range from £4 to £6 per call. In some instances all calls are charged at this rate, irrespective of a contact or sale being made via this call. It is easy to see on this cost basis how simple it is for costs to escalate unless firm parameters are given to the bureau on what is to be charged. This should become a subject for negotiation when drawing up a contract to work with a bureau. To help to control costs it is often safer to purchase operators on an hourly basis.

The efficacy of outbound telemarketing is usually calculated on the basis of the percentage of successful calls within the total of all calls made. A further measure is to calculate the conversion or sale rate of calls answered successfully – eg, of 100 calls made, 90 may have been answered but were unsuccessful; of the 'successful' 10, only 2 may convert to a sale, resulting in a 2 per cent sales conversion rate. Before entering into an outbound telemarketing campaign, the criteria by which its success is to be judged should be made clear to all involved.

As previously mentioned, outbound telemarketing appears to be more successful and acceptable as a tool in business-to-business marketing. It is a very cost-effective way of setting up appointments for sales representatives, as a sales device to customers who do not warrant a personal visit, etc. It has had considerable success when linked with other techniques, particularly direct mail. A letter could be used to set up a sales pitch and inform that a telephone call is to be expected. This technique has the effect of breaking down that initial reluctance barrier which can make some customers more receptive to the ensuing sales pitch.

Within business-to-business outbound telemarketing, the United Kingdom is used increasingly as a base for conducting international campaigns. This is due to both the high levels of expertise that now exist in some bureaux and the falling costs of international calls which has made the UK more competitive. There are some bureaux that follow daytime around the world and thus operate on a 24-hour basis.

The Direct Marketing Association in conjunction with the Director General of Fair Trading have developed guidelines for those conducting outbound telemarketing which are included in the DMA Code of Practice. A summary of these recommendations is given below.

Guidelines for outbound telemarketing

❑ **Disclosure** Callers must give the name of the company on whose behalf the call is being made. This information must be volunteered promptly and it should be repeated at any time that it is requested. The purpose of the must be stated early and the content of the call restricted to that purpose. If the call is being made as a result of a referral of a third party, that and the source must be disclosed, the caller having the opportunity to hang up.

❏ *Honesty* Telephone marketers must not mislead or evade the truth, and should answer the questions fully to the best of the knowledge available. Sales and marketing calls must not be disguised as research.

❏ *Reasonable hours* Calls should not be made during hours that are unreasonable to the recipient. Unless otherwise stated, calls should be made between 8am and 9pm. Recipients of calls should be asked if it is a convenient time and, if not, they should be called back.

❏ *Courtesy and procedures* High-pressure harassment tactics are to be avoided. Information, orders or appointments should not be solicited from minors. If an appointment is set, a contact number should be given so that the appointment can be cancelled, if desired.

❏ *Restriction of contacts* Called numbers should not be generated randomly or used knowingly if they are ex-directory or unlisted. The rules of the Telephone Preference Service should be followed.

For further details, the Direct Marketing Association Code of Practice should be consulted. A contact address and telephone number are included in the Appendix.

CUSTOMER CARE LINES

This is another area of growth within both outbound and inbound telemarketing. A quiet revolution has been taking place during the 'caring 90s' for companies both large and small to provide a telephone contact number. A leading telemarketing agency, the L&R Group, reports that the proportion of care line numbers on 'main brands' has risen from 8 to 22 per cent in just two years. From this research it appears that care lines have entered our culture rapidly. 26 per cent of those surveyed claim to have used already a care line at a time when they have only been available for a few years.

Customer care is, of course, a two way process and an area that is becoming a key focus within communication strategies, irrespective of the business sector. This is an area that outbound telemarketing in particular is ideally suited to. A call from a shop or supplier post purchase to check that all is well is likely to be extremely well received and is totally consistent with a proactive customer care strategy. This is a potentially powerful tool in 'relationship-building' strategies.

Customer care lines are a powerful tool to build up a good relationship with your customers.

THE TELEPHONE PREFERENCE SERVICE

This service was set up in January 1995. It offers consumers the same option with the telephone that they have with direct mail through the

Mailing Preference Service. Consumers can register their telephone number if they do not want to receive sales and marketing calls from companies with which they do not have an on-going contractual relationship. It is funded by annual subscriptions paid by companies who register to use the file. The larger the business, the greater is their allocated subscription. Registering for the scheme is free to consumers. Both British Telecom and Mercury have a toll-free information service for those who wish to register.

The Telephone Preference Service is voluntary and relies on the maximum number of outbound marketing companies to register in order to be effective. The bodies represented on the Telephone Preference Service board who will enforce the service are drawn from key industry sectors using the medium of outbound telemarketing – British Telecom, the Consumers Association, the Direct Marketing Association, the Glass and Glazing Federation, the Institute of Charity Fundraising Managers, Mercury Communications, the Periodical Publishers Association, and Oftel's Advisory Committee on Telecommunications for Small Businesses.

Chapter 9

Mail Order and Direct Selling

The definition of mail order to be discussed in this chapter is of home-based catalogue shopping which usually operates with or without an agent. It is a very fine line that divides this form of shopping from the related area of direct selling in which goods are sold direct in the customer's home.

MAIL ORDER – TRADITIONAL

Mail order has its origins in the USA. Large mail order empires developed and grew to satisfy the demands for products in the extensive rural markets that only had access to shops that provided the staples rather than the luxuries of life. One of the best known catalogues ever produced was that by the Sears Roebuck Corporation. In its heyday it was claimed to be the second most popular book in the world after the Bible!

Mail order had similarly been available in the UK from the 19th century, but the impetus for its growth came with the ready provision of credit in the catalogues developed during the 1930s. Repayments for goods could be made over an agreed period of time. This had great attractions during the early part of this century when disposable income was more limited, particularly among the working class. Purchasing from catalogues for many became an accepted practice if not the norm. Traditionally, catalogue shopping was conducted via an agent who acted on behalf of the catalogue. The agent would leave the catalogue, with customers allowing them to choose goods at their own convenience at home. The agent would place orders, distribute the goods and also chase repayments, usually on a weekly basis. As a reward for acting as an intermediary, the agent would be rewarded with commission or discount off goods in the catalogue. For some agents this acted to supplement the household income and some even made a comfortable living as an agent. The establishment of mail order as a working-class phenomenon has been difficult for the mail order industry to shake off. The traditional pattern of mail order behaviour is still practised, but there has been a shift towards individual rather than agent-based catalogue usage.

As credit is now easy and relatively cheap to obtain from many different sources, the credit rationale for catalogues could be thought to have diminished. There are still many who choose mail order as a way to shop, despite the relatively high rates of interest that are charged by some catalogues, as it is viewed as a more acceptable and discreet means of obtaining credit. With the general and non-stigmatised availability of credit, this is no longer the key motivator to purchase by mail order. Thus

Table 9.1   *Leading general mail order houses and their main catalogues, 1995*

Company	Parent	Main catalogues
Great Universal Stores PLC		Choice Family Album Great Universal Kays Marshall Ward Style Plus
Littlewoods Organisation PLC		Brian Mills Burlington Janet Frazer John Moores Littlewoods Peter Craig Special Edition
Freemans PLC	Sears	Freemans Editions Complete Essentials
Grattan PLC	Otto Versand	Grattan Look Again Grattan Direct
Empire Stores PLC	La Redoute	Empire La Redoute
N. Brown		Just For You Ambrose Wilson Candid Fashion World Heather Valley J D Williams Oxendale Classic Combination

Source: Trade interviews/Key Note

the emphasis has shifted the focus more on to the goods which are available.

Within the UK the mail order market is still dominated by the large general mail order companies although in-roads are being made by the smaller specialist operators. The 'Big Five', as they are often referred to, are thought to account for over 90 per cent of all general mail order business. The main players are Great Universal Stores, Littlewoods, Grattan, Freemans and Empire Stores. All of these operators have a range of catalogues that offer a wide selection of goods, but the majority of their sales is accounted for by clothing. The titles that the main mail order houses currently produce are detailed in Table 9.1 opposite.

There is a far from even split in the way that the business is shared among these operators. In terms of the value of sales that the operators account for, the market is dominated by Great Universal Stores and Littlewoods (see Table 9.2 below).

Table 9.2   *UK market shares of the mail order market by value, 1995*

Company	% Value
Great Universal Stores	35
Littlewoods	21
Freemans	12
Grattan	11
Empire Stores	7
N. Brown	6
Other	8
Total	100

Source: Key Note/company annual reports

It is thought that while mail order catalogues are in a dominant position, the relative sales of the main operators is coming under increasing pressure. The general retail environment within which the mail order houses compete is now more competitive, there has been a growth of other direct selling techniques which will be discussed later in the chapter, and there has been an increase in the number of smaller, more specialist catalogues. Some of these smaller catalogues do not compete directly with the large mail order houses but have none the less grown relatively, and potentially could steal a share within the total market.

The main operators have fought back by offering 'exclusive' ranges within their catalogues. Often produced for them by leading designers – eg, these exclusive lines have been the Vivienne Westwood and Workers For Freedom ranges in the Littlewoods catalogue. In addition, some houses

– eg, Freemans – are trying on the use of new media such as interactive television and the use of CD-i to display their merchandise, thus bringing the products to a potentially new audience. By using such new media, the image of the traditional catalogues is likely to be perceived as less boring and traditional.

Key Note Publications estimated that the general mail order business was valued at £4.7 billion in 1995 which, while substantial, has grown recently at a level below the average of total retail sales. This is a trend which is likely to continue as the competition in and outside this sector grows. The leading operators are likely to continue to play a role within the mail order sector, but it is likely that their business base will come under attack from all areas of retailing, mail order and direct selling.

MAIL ORDER – NEW GENERATION

In the recent past there has been a rapid expansion in the number and diversity of goods that are available through mail order. This trend was given impetus in the UK with the advent of the Next Directory in 1988. The product offering was initially an extension of that offered in its stores – a stylish, quality product. There was a realisation in the market of the possibility of giving a mail order product more of a 'lifestyle' focus as opposed to the generalist product that was then available. In addition, the launch of the Next Directory helped to break down the perception that goods ordered via mail order were downmarket or second rate.

Since the late 1980s a plethora of upmarket and specialist mail order products have been launched – eg, Land's End, Racing Green and Boden operate in the clothing market, while The White Company brings a niche offering of household lines and goods with the single distinguishing feature of being available only in white! These are but a few of the many specialist operators that have entered the market and are being joined by new entrants on an almost weekly basis. It is now possible to buy products as diverse as spiked shoes to aerate a lawn to a limited edition piece of porcelain via mail order.

The growth of mail order is not restricted to consumer products – there have also been some interesting developments in the business-to-business sector. Amstrad, for example, announced in 1995 that it was to withdraw all of its products from the mainstream retail sector because of a dispute over margins/pricing with the retail trade. It switched its selling channels entirely to mail order/direct selling. Consumer brown goods such as satellite dishes and multi-media computers are available in addition to office products such as plain paper fax machines. The key benefit that Amstrad claims to offer by switching to a mail order/ direct selling base is that they are able to pass on the margins normally given to the retail trade directly to the customer in the form of reduced prices.

Viking Direct has established itself as a successful and efficient supplier of office products. This is a concept that is well established in the USA but has been a relatively new innovation in the UK. Already there has been an apparent growth in this sector – eg, W.H. Smith has introduced a competitive service in the form of its 'Nice Day' operation.

In addition to the improvement of the actual or perceived quality of the products on offer in mail order, there has been an improvement in the distribution system to deliver these products. Many mail order companies will guarantee next day delivery for certain items on payment of a premium delivery charge. Such a service reduces another potential negative of mail order shopping – deferred gratification.

The USA is often cited as a model to herald what may occur in the UK. We are currently estimated to be five to ten years behind the US mail order market. Regular catalogue buyers in the UK currently receive between five and ten catalogues a month. At this level mail order is thought to account for about 4 per cent of non-food retail sales. In the USA, between 50 and 60 catalogues are received by regular catalogue buyers, and it is predicted that non-food sales by catalogue could reach 50 per cent by the year 2000.

If such a growth rate is to be replicated in the UK, there will have to be a major proliferation in the number and diversity of catalogues available in the UK. In addition, they will have to be backed up by exceptional levels of service to conquer reluctant mail order customers. Growth will undoubtedly occur in this sector, but it is unlikely to be of the magnitude predicted in the USA. The development of database management techniques as discussed in Chapter 6 will undoubtedly help with the growth of this more specialist arm of the mail order sector. It is feasible that specialist business bases could be expanded through the judicious use of tailor-made mailing lists that use existing customers as a predictive model for locating new customers.

> There is an enormous potential for growth in the mail order market in the UK.

DIRECT SELLING

Direct selling is a newer form of shopping compared to general mail order. The distinctions between them are somewhat blurred, but they are characterised by involving one-to-one selling in the customer's home by a distributor acting on behalf of the company. Direct selling is not a single discipline. Three main methods are used: single level selling, network or pyramid selling and party plans.

❑ **Single level selling** A distributor will demonstrate a product in someone's home or will leave a catalogue. The distributor is responsible for taking the order and for delivering the goods. Betterware is a typical example of this form of selling operation.

❑ **Network selling** The structure of the sales force differs in this operation. Independent distributors generate income through recruiting sellers as well as generating their own direct sales. Distributors are able to earn income on their own sales as well as those sales generated by their recruits. From the customer's standpoint, the selling relationship is identical to single level selling – until an attempt is made to recruit them on to the sales force! This type of selling operation has come under criticism in the past, especially as sales territories become saturated.

❑ **Party plan** This form of selling is for products that are easy to demonstrate in a social setting. They are generally relatively low ticket items – usually less than £25. The distributors are responsible for arranging parties in their own homes or in other people's homes. Customers who are willing to stage parties benefit in receiving free goods or discounts off purchases. The majority of these companies specialise in one or two product lines – eg, Ann Summers (lingerie), Usborne (books and games).

These areas of direct marketing have experienced dramatic growth rates. Key Note Publications estimated that in 1995, sales in this area were £1 billion. One of the principal reasons for the growth in direct selling is due to the economic environment. The recession of the early 1990s made many people redundant and in need of alternative employment. Some of the opportunities in this area are ideal for those who are seeking alternative self-employed careers. They are also suitable for people seeking to supplement their household income by working part-time from home.

In order for this category to continue to grow, it will need to recruit more individuals as sales people and also to offer differentiated products that are not available through other channels. The success of the Tupperware party plan operation is arguably due to quality products (they carry lifetime guarantees), but importantly they are not available through any other distribution channel. Cabouchon, the costume jewellery company as followed these principles and has established an extremely successful business.

FUTURE DEVELOPMENTS IN HOME SHOPPING

In addition to the developments in new technology that will be discussed in greater depth in Chapter 12, some developments are taking place in the UK retail scene which may have major implications for the future.

The advent of home grocery shopping, while once commonplace via the local grocer and delivery boy, is still largely unavailable and unaffordable to the masses who cannot afford to shop at Harrods. Many localised trials have taken place by the major multiples to check the feasibility of this concept, but such services are not yet available nationally.

Within the USA several direct grocery delivery services have been set up and appear to be operating successfully. Many are expanding their business. Two of the key players are:

- **Peapod** This is available in Chicago, San Francisco and will soon be expanded to Boston. Shoppers use a software program from home via a modem. The groceries are hand packed and delivered to the customer's home in temperature controlled bins. There is a membership cost and a minimum order threshold.
- **Shoppers Express** This has been established for 8 years, using 32 grocery chains in 40 major cities. It is mainly catalogue based with a telephone ordering system.

Limited tests have been conducted by Somerfield and Tesco, but the most interesting service to date is being conducted via Sainsbury's. A company called Flanagans started trading in October 1995 in south London. They offer a home delivery service on 2,500 lines available in Sainsbury's. Telephone or fax ordering is made via selection from a 128-page colour catalogue which contains product lists, visuals and instructions. It is rumoured that this company may be rebranded as Sainsbury Direct. While currently a small operation, it could represent the next phase in the 'grocery wars' to help Sainsbury reclaim its market leadership role. Tesco have announced a test market with a similar service in Ealing, west London. Such developments would be totally consistent as an extension of the 'quality of service' strategies which have become the current battleground of the grocery multiples.

Home delivery of groceries via the telephone is the next development in the direct selling field.

There have been other growth areas in the direct selling field which are likely to grow in the future, take away food delivery being a case in

point. Ten years ago pizza, curries and Chinese food were largely purchased in restaurants or in supermarkets to cook at home. The
introduction of pizza delivery through companies such as Domino's has
started a trend among restaurants to offer a delivery service to accompany
an existing take-away service.

Chapter 10
Door-to-Door

Door-to-door is usually defined as non-personalised and non-addressed sales literature that is delivered via the letterbox. The most common types of material to be delivered are leaflets, coupons and samples. Door-to-door admittedly lacks the glamour of communication techniques such as television advertising but nevertheless it has a role to play within integrated communication plans.

Door-to-door has many real benefits:

❑ *Targeting* It is possible to target a door drop on many different criteria – by television area, region, town and importantly by geodemographic profile.

❑ *Reach* The number of households to be communicated with can be calculated accurately. It is also the only medium with the ability to target all households in the UK without duplication.

❑ *Integration* For maximum effect, door-drops in whatever form should be integrated fully with the other communication tools.

❑ *Detail* It is possible to include complex messages if this is deemed appropriate – eg, the Central Office of Information selected door-to-door as one of the communication channels to educate people about Aids awareness. It is more flexible than alternative media – ie, television and posters that are only geared to take simple, short messages.

❑ *Impact* If appropriately novel, a door-drop can demand to be read.

❑ *Cost efficiency* This is one of the cheapest forms of communication available.

❑ *Database building* It is possible to use it as a device to collect basic research data or names and addresses, all of which can be included on a database for future use.

❑ *Timing* It is possible to field campaigns with relatively short lead times.

❑ *Efficacy* Door-drops of coupons are estimated by Nielsen to have higher redemption levels. In magazines and newspapers, redemption levels are 2 and 3 per cent respectively, compared with 12 per cent in door-drops.

❑ *In-store traffic generation* Door-drops of information leaflets/coupons are a proven method of increasing localised in-store traffic.

Door-to-door thus has much to offer as a communication medium. It is widely used by both large and small companies. It is currently estimated that four times as many door-drops are received than direct mail shots indicating that many businesses are aware of the benefits it offers.

In developing a door-to-door campaign, the following issues need to be considered:

❑ What is to be delivered?
❑ To whom is it to be delivered?
❑ How will it be delivered?
❑ What checks should be made to validate delivery?
❑ How much will it cost?

WHAT IS TO BE DELIVERED?

The first decision to be made concerns what is to be put through the letterbox. Unlike direct mail, there are fewer restrictions on the physical characteristics of items to be delivered. Common sense dictates that it must be a suitable shape to fit through a letterbox and be an appropriate weight sympathetic to the delivery medium – ie, it should not be too heavy. If sample products are bulky or heavy, it is preferable to develop smaller sample packs for delivery.

The creative material – whether it is a leaflet, a coupon or a combination of both – should be developed carefully to maximise its impact. It is potentially a very short journey from the doormat to the bin! Every effort should be made to ensure that at the very least the message is communicated en route. Door-drop creative material needs to be visually demanding to achieve an impact. Each element should be treated like an advertisement; single-minded benefits should be communicated. Whatever the creative execution selected, ensure that it remains consistent with other creative material being used in the communication mix to reap the benefits of integrated communication.

There is much creative freedom in developing material for door-drops to maximise their impact. Devices such as cut-out shapes, which are not feasible to be sent by mail, can be used for added interest. Teasers or front covers of leaflets work to draw the customer in to read the rest of the message.

Despite the apparent advantage that door-drops can convey detailed information, this may be highly inappropriate for some products or services as there is a risk that it looks too complicated and hence will be discarded immediately.

TO WHOM IS IT TO BE DELIVERED?

The target audience for a door drop can be defined as loosely or as tightly as is desired. For some products or services the target may be relatively easy to define – eg, all households within a ten-minute drive time of a store. For other products or services it may be more appropriate to use more complex targeting techniques. The more involved the target defi-nition, the more costly it is likely to be to reach them. The use of targeting, however, has increased the attraction of door-to-door as a communication technique as there is reassurance about the nature of the recipient of a door-drop.

The techniques most frequently used are based on those used in direct mail – ie, geodemographics. The main operators in this sector – Acorn, Mosaic, Superprofiles and Define – all offer analysis of areas to help to reach predefined targets. See Chapter 6 for a fuller explanation of these services. In addition, the Association of Household Distributors has recently developed its own system called the AHD Property Classification. This classification goes down to a delivery-round level of an average 250 households, describes the predominant housing type, location in town or city, and the age of the property. Only members of the AHD have access to this classification system.

The targeting of door-drops can never be as precise as the service provided by direct mail, but the developments in the application of geode-mographic techniques provide reassurance that the messages are not entirely mismatched.

HOW IS IT TO BE DELIVERED?

Three principal bodies deliver door-drops – the Royal Mail, specialist distribution companies and free newspapers. The choice of distribution channel will be an individual one, depending on the targeting requirements, areas to be covered, nature of the door-drop and the budget available.

The Royal Mail unaddressed delivery service is subject to the same standards as the regular mail and is delivered by the same network of uniformed postmen and women. It provides access to 24 million letterboxes in the 8,900 postcode sectors throughout the UK. It is the most flexible of the delivery options as the day of delivery can be specified.

Ensure that your chosen distribution service is monitored and approved by an outside organisation.

If a distribution specialist company is used, ensure that they are members of the AHD. Membership of this body ensures that they have agreed to certain operating standards and a monitored code of practice.

Similarly, if a free newspaper is used for your door-drop, ensure that its circulation is monitored by the Verified Free Newspaper Distribution (VFD), a division of the Audited Bureau of Circulation (ABC), which checks that circulation figures are as claimed. This method of delivery can cover 86 per cent of the country, reaching 18 million households. It has the advantage of guaranteeing delivery, usually over a three-day period in any week of the year.

After selecting the distribution channel, the next decision to be made is whether to send the door-drop solus or shared. The obvious advantage of a solus door-drop is that the impact is maximised because it will be the only promotional material being delivered at that time. This technique can also be enhanced further by combining it with a personal call. This is particularly suitable for delivering samples and collecting basic research data. This technique is known as 'knock and drop'. On the negative side, solus delivery is obviously the most expensive option as costs cannot be shared.

The main distributors offer shared distribution, or 'shareplan' as it is referred to. Omnibus deliveries of non-competing items are made every month. Usually up to four items are delivered at any one time. The delivery time can be over a three-week period and hence may not be suitable if timing is critical to tie in with other activities. Items are delivered by adult teams.

WHAT CHECKS SHOULD BE MADE TO VALIDATE DELIVERY?

The best way to validate delivery is through back-checking. This system is offered for an additional fee by the distribution companies which make calls post-delivery and report on the level of receipt and recall. If a more objective validation is required, a specialist independent research company will need to be employed. The research company will define statistically representative clusters of households and carry out interviews with the residents. Such validation is only cost effective on large-scale door-drops in excess of five million.

HOW MUCH WILL IT COST?

The costs that can be incurred when using door-to-door split into three categories: strategic, media, print and production.

Strategic costs for coupon redemption or data capture will depend on the nature of the campaign and may not even be incurred in some instances. Allowance should be made for redemption, clearing house fees and retailer handling fees if coupons are used. Clearance house fees start at £13 per thousand and retailer handling fees are £26.50 per thousand.

The media or distribution costs are influenced by the size/weight of the door-drop, the quantity, distribution area, whether distributed solus or shared, targeting specifications, and which supplier is used. Media costs in door-to-door have increased very little in comparison to those of other media. In real terms it is now cheaper to undertake door-to-door than it was in the early 1980s because of increased competition and low pay rates for distributors. Guideline costs are as follows: solus distribution starts at £27 per thousand, shareplan at £11 per thousand and news share at £12 per thousand. Targeting starts at £2 per thousand but increases the more complex the target specification is. If validation research is required, costs for this service start from £2 per validation.

Print and production costs similarly are dependent on the nature of the creative vehicle that has been developed. Economies of scale do operate but only after a certain critical mass has been exceeded; thereafter costs have a tendency to stabilise. As a guideline on costs, to produce one million colour A4 sheets costs in the region of £10 per thousand and sample production costs start at £200 per thousand.

As with many of the other tools of direct marketing, thorough planning of door-to-door delivery at the outset will ensure that pitfalls are avoided, and the benefits of this cost-effective and positive communication channel will be reaped.

Chapter 11

Research Techniques in Direct Marketing

Research is used in direct marketing to provide guidance in the following areas:

❑ Developing creative material.
❑ Analysing creative material in test markets.
❑ Post campaign analysis to assess its effectiveness.

Both qualitative and quantitative methodologies can be used in these key stages of development. The choice of technique(s) is usually dependent on the task in hand. It is always wise to seek independent guidance from an outside agency or specialist research company to ensure that the most appropriate form of research has been selected. Any research conducted should be sure to follow the Market Research Society (MRS) Code of Conduct (their address is included in the Appendix). A brief guide to the most frequently used techniques is discussed in this chapter. It is not intended as a comprehensive guide to all the techniques that are available; rather it is an outline of the broad types of research that are available and proven to be appropriate to help campaign development and assessment.

Have your research conducted by a specialist company and ensure that it follows the MRS Code of Conduct.

DEVELOPING CREATIVE MATERIAL

Qualitative research is the most frequently used tool when creative work is being developed. This usually takes the form of concept development and creative assessment. The qualitative technique most often used initially is group discussions. If it is deemed necessary to have quantitative back-up for any qualitative findings, this is most often done via a questionnaire conducted in the street, home, or in a hall.

Group discussions involve recruiting a group of people who are representative of the target audience. To maximise the group dynamic – ie, to get people talking – it is usual to have between five and ten people in a group. If it is smaller than this number conversation is inhibited; if the group is larger, it becomes difficult for all the members to contribute. For some investigations into potentially sensitive or embarrassing topics, mini-groups of about three or four people, or individual in-depth interviews may be conducted.

Group discussions are moderated and guided by an experienced researcher who ideally should be independent of the company that has been responsible for developing the creative work. This ensures that objectivity is maintained. The moderator elicits from the people taking part in the group discussion which ideas they find the most motivating and gives guidance on improvements that could be made to maximise the efficacy of the creative work.

Group discussions are most frequently used in direct marketing for concept development and to help in the development of creative work. They are also useful to gain an insight into the characteristics and behaviour of the target market. This target audience information can be incorporated into the creative brief. Concept development involves presenting the group with a series of single-minded thoughts, positioning or promotional devices, usually accompanied by a visual. At the end of the concept research, it should be clear what the most motivating way would be to position the product or service to be promoted via direct marketing. The concept research usually results in the creative brief, which is discussed in depth in Chapter 5.

The creative work that evolves from the creative brief can be assessed similarly using group discussions. This is particularly useful if the creative team which produces the work has alternative executions, or if there is indecision about the preferred creative route. As many of the areas of direct marketing are developing rapidly, direct mail in particular, it is vital to keep in tune with the increasing sophistication of the target audience.

Qualitative research is in some ways a more sensitive tool than quantitative research as it is able to give guidance on key aspects such as the tonal values of the execution, elements that motivate and those that demotivate, as well as simple likes and dislikes.

If quantitative research is used, questionnaires should be designed carefully to gain an objective response. The length of the questionnaire and its complexity will determine the location in which it should be conducted. If it is short, interviewing is possible in the street. If it is long and involves many open-ended questions, it is more usual for them to be conducted in the home or a hall. These locations are preferred for practical reasons such as comfort or the ability to show creative material.

Quantitative research is most usually used at the end of the creative development process to give numerical results; most usually it is a means of deciding between alternative executions. It is dangerous to use only quantitative research in the decision-making process as it can only tell you which execution works – it cannot explain why.

ANALYSING CREATIVE MATERIAL IN TEST MARKETS

Direct marketing tools are unique because they are totally discreet. They are the only methods available that can be tested in a controlled environment to assess the relative efficiencies of alternative approaches. It is possible to run test markets in direct mail, telemarketing or door-to-door.

For companies which are new to these techniques, it is particularly useful to run test markets if the likely response rates are an unknown quantity. The size of the test market will be determined by the nature of the direct marketing tool to be used and the method of assessing its effectiveness. In some instances it is possible to use an area as small as a town; in other cases, more robust data may be needed, in which case larger areas such as a television or marketing region may need to be used. There is a school of thought that says that an alternative execution should always be selected and run alongside the main execution as it is only through such initiatives that learning in the market can occur.

Test marketing in direct marketing is relatively straightforward. The following procedures should be followed:

❑ Select the area(s) to be researched.
❑ Conduct any pre-studies, if they are appropriate, to ensure that base data exists with which research results can be compared.
❑ Field the research.
❑ Analyse the response by the appropriate measures – usually a combination of quantitative and qualitative techniques will provide the most relevant data.
❑ Decide which is the optimum approach and replicate it on a larger scale.

This form of test marketing is used in the development of direct mail campaigns in particular. It is used to change systematically various elements of a campaign to determine the optimum package. There is virtually no limit to the number of tests that you can run in direct mail because the mailing can be split up into many segments. The main limiting constraint on how many options are tested is likely to be cost. Ensure that when different options in various segments are being tested, there is only one change in the variable versus a 'control', which is the master mail-shot that the other options being tested must try to beat, otherwise it will be impossible to isolate the most effective elements that are being tested.

The types of alternatives that can be tested are as follows:

❑ *Product or service* This helps to determine what you should be offering in a direct mail campaign.
❑ *Lists* More than one list may be available or you may wish to test a new list versus the one that you use currently. This can help to determine the most effective list for future use.
❑ *Price* Test at different price levels or the redemption levels of coupons to see which produces the most cost-effective level of response.
❑ *Incentives* There may be alternative 'gimmicks' or incentives that can be used – eg, a competition versus a money-off coupon. Always be sure to test against an option without an incentive as it may not be necessary at all.
❑ *Timing* Is there an optimum time for the campaign in terms of season-ality in the market? Should it precede, coincide with or follow other marketing activity if it is part of an integrated campaign?
❑ *Frequency* How often should mailings be sent out? Is there an optimum spacing to achieve relationship building or a sales effect?
❑ *Creative work* It is possible for totally different creative approaches to be researched or simply to research different elements of a consistent creative approach – eg, long versus a short letter, plain versus a decorated envelope, etc.

POST-CAMPAIGN ANALYSIS

The techniques of post-campaign analysis are many and varied. Which techniques should be selected will be determined by the initial objectives of the direct marketing campaign. At its most basic, simple numerical measures are useful to check how effective the response rates were. At the other dimension, it is possible to conduct complex tracking studies to help to understand how your propositions are faring over time. Which methods to select is largely determined on the budgets that are available. Those with more modest budgets would be ill-advised to conduct no more than rudimentary post-campaign research; those with large-scale expenditure may be more prudent to conduct research on a larger scale to verify that direct marketing is performing as desired – eg, tracking studies.

A word of caution on any post-campaign analysis is appropriate. Many direct marketing techniques are 'slow burn' in their effect, so research measures may not pick up changes in behaviour immediately.

Simple numerical methods will analyse campaign effectiveness by parameters such as:

❑ *Response rates* This is usually expressed as the percentage of the total mailed. If 100 were mailed and 5 responded, the response rate would be 5 per cent.
❑ *The cost per response* This is calculated by dividing the cost of the direct marketing activity by the number of people who responded. If in the above example it cost £200 to mail the 100 prospective customers, the cost per response would be £40.
❑ *Conversion rates* If a multi-stage selling process is in operation, this is the proportion of the initial respondents who eventually buy a product or service.
❑ *Cost per sale* Again, in multi-stage selling a response alone may not be the end of the story; it will be the net result of perhaps many communications that eventually result in a sale.

Other methods of analysis post-campaign can be either qualitative, quantitative or a combination of both. Qualitative research could give guidance on shifts in attitude or perception that have occurred since the campaign began. Group discussions conducted after the campaign is finished among known recipients of the material would be a suitable technique. It can be quantitative also. Telephone research is a useful tool to provide basic quantitative data – eg, on likes, dislikes, impact, propensity to purchase, etc.

Both of these methodologies should be conducted in close proximity to the campaign activity as memories are notoriously short when it comes to recalling some direct marketing material. It should be noted that such research is equally useful in assessing reasons why a campaign failed to perform as well as had been expected. These forms of research are suitable for campaigns both large and small as they can be tailored easily to fit individual budgets.

Keep up to date with ideas and strategies by conducting research after a campaign.

It is strongly recommended that research is conducted after a campaign has finished. It is only by constantly up-dating knowledge that ideas and strategies are able to evolve, develop and progress. It is tempting to relax once a campaign has 'gone to bed', but this should be regarded as the start of the next phase of development, not just the end of a campaign.

Tracking studies have been mentioned as a means of assessing campaign effectiveness. These are larger scale studies that dip into the market at regular intervals to check shifts in attitudes, recall of marketing activity and purchasing behaviour for a given product or service. They need to run over a period of time to provide a bank of data that can be used to track shifts on any of the predetermined scales. They are most commonly used by large advertisers who wish to track what happens before and after campaigns. As expenditure in certain areas of direct marketing now rivals that in some sectors of advertising, it is likely that this may be used more in the future as a research technique to refine direct marketing campaigns.

Chapter 12
New Marketing Communication Opportunities

Such is the rate of change and development of some of the newer tools of marketing communication that information in this chapter may be out of date already! Some of the areas to be discussed are not yet in mainstream use but have the potential to be of great importance in the future. It is an area which is surrounded with a certain amount of hype and mystery. Topics to be covered include:

❑ The Internet.
❑ Compact disc technology.
❑ Interactive kiosks.
❑ Interactive television.

THE INTERNET

Until a few years ago only computer enthusiasts were aware of or had access to the Internet. In a short time it has been transformed *apparently* to a mainstream communication tool. The Internet is now much in evidence in marketing communications – ie, no self-respecting advertiser would run an advertisement without a ubiquitous 'website' reference.

The Internet does not exist as a single entity – it is a network of computer networks that are able to communicate with each other. It expands as each new 'subscriber' joins the service. It is relatively easy to become connected to the Internet by purchasing the appropriate computer, a modem to link between the computer and the telephone, and then subscribing to access via a service provider. Depending on which piece of research is consulted, it is estimated that people with access to the Internet could be anything from 30 to 60 million on a worldwide basis.

Growth in the number of people with access to the Internet is likely to continue. Within the UK, the £300 computer system is in sight. This is judged to be the price 'trigger point' which will lead to penetration levels that will grow in line with numbers now achieved by the video recorder.

In addition, it is rumoured that new technology will be launched in 1996–97 which will provide access to the Internet without the need for a computer. This new 'box of tricks' is able to access the Internet in the usual way via a telephone link and to download the desired information which is then played back through the domestic television. Specially adapted hand-sets are used to enable interaction with the information displayed on the television screen.

A brief history

The Internet began in 1969 as a small network of computers as a project of the US Department of Defence. It was originally called 'Arpanet'. By the early 1970s academics had seized upon it as a way of sending information to each other. The 'Internet' was 'officially' created in 1973. By 1982 it had 1000 users worldwide. Gradually, the community of people using the Internet has grown, exponentially. It should be noted that nobody owns the Internet; similarly, nobody controls it. Hence, some of the services which are readily accessible to all have been the subject of much criticism – eg, pornography.

Using the Internet

Two basic rules have been drawn up by the Internet Committee, a self-appointed user group in the USA, for those who wish to advertise on the Internet:

❑ Advertising should be passive, allowing the Internet to come to the advertising rather than the advertiser imposing their message on the user. Abusing this rule, by sending messages to users, is likely to result in users sending large volumes of e-mail to clog the sender's computer.

❑ Advertising should offer factual information rather than hyperbole.

There are thus limits in the way that the Internet could be used in direct marketing – it would be unlikely to become an electronic replacement for direct mail, for instance. The protocol for using the Internet may, of course, change over time, which would warrant a review of this situation.

There are numerous examples of companies using the Internet but currently there are no *published* examples of its proven marketing efficacy in comparison with other communication tools. There are some users who have very simple information-based pages. It can be argued that these provide little in the way of a reward for those who have taken the trouble to seek out the website. There needs to be a constant appraisal of the way in which information is presented on the Internet as it is developing so rapidly that devices such as a filling up a Guinness glass, which was used on the first advertisement-led website in the UK, are already passé.

Advertisers such as Mars Snickers that have used the medium in a new, interactive way have opened new horizons in communication methodology. They have developed a youth-oriented magazine format, 'Snickers Mega-bite', that is regularly updated and whose content is 'controlled' by those who access the site.

As this is such a new communication channel, the onus is on the marketing community to find the ways and means of maximising its potential.

The Internet and direct marketing

At first sight the Internet may seem to be of limited use in direct marketing because of its apparent limitations as a conduit for commercial direct mail, for example. It is very difficult to predict absolutely how the Internet may evolve eventually as a direct marketing tool, but there are indicators in the market that hint at the way its undoubted strengths may be harnessed. As it is a relatively low-cost medium to exploit, many companies are testing it for direct marketing purposes.

The areas in which it appears to have limited success in direct marketing are:

❑ Database building.
❑ Mail order.

Database building

Many commercial advertisers on the Internet have developed their communication to provide an opportunity for the user to feed back information. This not only rewards the user for seeking out the site but it can also be tailored as a means of gathering information about those people who are accessing the site. It is likely that many people are using this data for developing and refining databases.

Mail order

This area has obvious attractions as goods can be displayed without the need to distribute a catalogue. The main inhibitor for growth in this area is the lack of security when transactions are made direct via the Internet. Until this problem is resolved, this area is unlikely to grow at a rapid pace. Innovations has a mail order service for a standard range of goods. Tesco has a national service for wines and is currently testing a full grocery range in Ealing, West London.

Advertising on the Internet

There are four key stages to gain access to the Interenet as an advertising medium:

1. *Concept* Have a clear idea what you want to do and why, and try to adapt to what the net has to offer. Stolichnaya have used the Internet to provide brand entertainment with an interactive bias. There is almost too much that can be done on the Internet and without a clear focus the result could be chaotic.
2. *Creation* Once you know what your site is aiming to do, you have to decide its structure and what it is going to look like. It is the equivalent of a 3-D storyboard set up for approval. Putting up a website is very different from organising traditional media. The web is based on hypertext which allows you to point, click and move swiftly between pages in any order you want. Good sites allow you to move around easily without going back to a home page.
3. *Production* Websites are written in a programming language called HTML. You may also want to include other programmes, such as a response mechanism on e-mail.
4. *Placement* Where do you put the advertisement? Three main options are open:

   - On-line publications – eg, HotWired, FutureNet, Electronic Tele-graph or Times.
   - Space can be hired on a server. This would give you your own address and the ability to include sponsorship banners or links on other sites. This allows people to click on to your logo and then to be whisked off to your site.
   - Go for it alone! You will need to ensure that your address becomes

known – eg, by having your address listed on the Netscape What's New page.

Points to avoid for your Internet site

❑ *No one can find it* It is all well and good putting up a site, but unless someone knows how to find it, there is no point in being there. Even if you are connected to an on-line journal, it is advisable to put out a press release to all the relevant trade, consumer and Internet titles. Also, you should try to get links to your site on the Netscape What's New site and a listing in the Yahoo directory, plus any other relevant sites.

❑ *Enormous graphics take an eternity to download* No one minds waiting for something that they really want, but having to wait an eternity while your corporate logo appears will make the browser turn off. Make sure that you see your site on-line rather than check it on a hard disk which makes things appear much faster. Preferably, check your site by using a computer linked to a standard 14.4k modem.

❑ *Response mechanisms that don't work* If you let people send e-mail to you, make sure that you get something back quickly. In some cases this may be a waste of time as it involves too much effort. It may be more appropriate to use telemarketing to handle responses.

❑ *Poor architecture* A website is best seen as a 3-D construction and if people are to like it they will to have to get around it quickly and intuitively.

❑ *Intrusive registration* You can ask people to register for your site by filling in a form. However, don't take liberties. If e-mail addresses are requested, reassure the enquirer that he or she will not be passed on for unsolicited mail.

Don't hide your Internet site – advertise yourself well in the relevant journals.

The Internet has gained such prominence in the minds of marketing people that it is unlikely to go away. How it will *actually* be used in the future is very hard to gauge and it may be foolhardy to try to predict its future path. It is unlikely ever to achieve the coverage levels of television because not everyone is computer literate nor does everyone have access to a computer. It is an extremely fragmented medium so it is likely that some messages are never received. If it is ever to be a truly mainstream rather than a niche medium, the current target audience needs to expand beyond its current male and youth bias towards a profile that is more representative of society as a whole.

The ultimate curb throughout its use in most of the world, excluding the USA, in a domestic situation is likely to be the cost of access. Until

oll-free local calls are available, the growth of the Internet could poten-
ially stop dead in its tracks. The current cost of regular or prolonged use
s largely prohibitive for the mass market.

The attractions of the Internet as a potential local or global direct
marketing tool are in theory very potent. However, it is likely that the
nternet may develop as a direct marketing tool in ways that we are not
et aware of. After all, although Marconi developed the radio to allow two
people to communicate; its use is now totally different from its original
intention. The same phenomenon may well occur with the Internet.

The potential of the Internet as a direct marketing tool, both locally and globally, is enormous, although its future course is unknown.

COMPACT DISC TECHNOLOGY

Two forms of compact disc are relevant to direct marketing – the CD-i
and the CD-Rom.

The CD-i was originally developed by Philips as a stand-alone system
for interactive information and educational use in the home. It is usually
played through a domestic television set via a CD-i player. The CD-i has
evolved and is more likely to be used for computer games than for anything
else in the home.

There have been trials to provide a home-shopping facility on CD-i.
The most notable trial of this was a joint venture conducted by Barclays
Bank, Page & Moy travel company, and Freemans catalogue company.
CD-i owners were mailed three home-shopping CDs, one from each
participant and orders were made over the telephone. This has been an
interesting development but the growth of this form of direct marketing
will be limited by the penetration of the players who are necessary to play
the CD-i. It is likely that this form of direct marketing will be unlikely
to grow as the CD-i may be taken over by the CD-ROM.

The CD-ROM has grown dramatically in the recent past. It differs
from CD-i in that it is played via a computer. Owing to the rapid
growth of multi-media computer systems in the UK, this area has become
increasingly attractive as a direct marketing communications medium for
consumer and business-to-business markets alike.

CD-Roms can be used to produce 'live' catalogues with audio
accompaniment. Their ability to demonstrate products in the home or
office potentially could be of great interest. Barclays Bank have even
developed a version of CD-ROM as part of an interactive staff-training
programme.

New ways of using this flexible medium are being developed all the time. It is likely that we have not yet even scratched the surface of the way in which it could be used in direct marketing.

INTERACTIVE KIOSKS

Interactive kiosks are usually computer systems, located in public place which inform about and/or sell products via a screen display which the user controls. The main systems that are used are CD-ROMS linked up to a computer system or less frequently a CD-i linked to a standard television set. A few small trials have taken place around the UK using this system. Interactive kiosks have not yet become either commonplace or fully accepted by customers as a usual conduit of information or as a means of purchasing. They have been relatively expensive communication vehicles to develop and this has acted as a limiting factor on their growth. As technology costs continue to fall in real terms, they are likely to become a more widespread direct marketing communication tool. Interactive kiosks potentially have many benefits:

- ❏ Instant provision of large amounts of information.
- ❏ A menu-driven selling system which tailors itself to the needs of the customer through their direct control of it.
- ❏ No staff requirements.
- ❏ Provision of consistent information at all times.
- ❏ In theory, the ability to be located anywhere.
- ❏ A direct response mechanism which allows customers to enter their names and addresses, to request more information, a brochure, etc.
- ❏ Direct selling off the screen using a swipe card facility.

INTERACTIVE TELEVISION

Interactive television is already on trial in the UK. Advances in technology have enabled television and cable companies to start to deliver interactive television in the home. It is heralded as a unique home entertainment, information education and shopping service all rolled into one. The facilities such as near programming on demand that interactive television offers, while an interesting media development, are not really of any relevance to direct marketing.

The area that may prove itself to be of more interest is the related home-shopping service that it provides. The British Telecom test which has taken place in 2500 homes in the Colchester area has an interactive High Street program. Participating retailers included Freemans, Adams, Selfridges Selection, Olympus Sports, W.H. Smith and Thomas Cook. Each 'shop' provides all the information needed to make a purchase. The information is provided via a combination of videos, still photographs and on-screen text-based information. Purchases are made direct by using a credit or debit card and the goods are delivered to the door. Thomas Cook operates differently as they will follow up with a telephone call to discuss details prior to booking.

Sky Television has a planned launch of their digital service which, in addition to providing over 250 channels, has the ability for an interactive service. The BBC similarly is committed to the provision of inter-active services.

It is likely that such a provision will be commonplace in the future and that our current static system of receiving programme information will appear somewhat 'quaint'. There is a real challenge for direct marketing to develop and embrace the opportunities that this dynamic medium may afford in the future.

Appendix

Advertising Standards Authority
Brook House
2–16 Torrington Place
London WC1E 7HN
Tel: 0171 580 5555

Association of Household
Distributors Limited
36 Frogmore Street
Tring
Hertfordshire HP23 5AU
Tel: 01442 890991

CACI Ltd
CACI House
Kensington Village
Avonmore Road
London W14 8TS
Tel: 0171 602 6000
e-mail : marketing@caci.co.uk

CCN/Mosaic
39 Houndsditch Road
London EC3A 5DB
Tel: 0171 623 5551

CDMS/Superprofiles
Kershaw Avenue
Crosby
Liverpool L23 OXA

CMT
Causeway House

The Causeway
Teddington
Middlesex TW11 OJR

Data Protection Registrar
Wycliffe House
Water Lane
Wilmslow
Cheshire SK9 5AF
Tel: 01625 545700

Direct Mail Information Service
5 Carlisle Street
London W1V 5RG
Tel: 0171 494 0483

Direct Marketing Association (UK)
    Ltd
Haymarket House
1 Oxendon Street
London SW1Y 4EE
Tel: 0171 321 2525

Equifax/Define
Capital House
25 Chapel Street
London NW1 5DS

ICD Marketing Services Ltd
Boundary House
91–93 Charterhouse Street
London EC1M 6HR

Institute of Direct Marketing
1 Park Road
Teddington
Middlesex TW11 OAR

Mailing Preference Service
5 Reef House
Plantation Wharf
London SW11 3UF

Mail Order Protection Scheme
16 Took's Court
London EC4 1LB

Market Research Society
15 Northburgh Street
London EC1V OAH

NDL
Port House
Square Rigger Road
Plantation Wharf
London SW1 3TY

Print and Publishers Association
Queens House
28 Kingsway
London WC2B 6JR

Royal Mail Customer Service Centres
(See telephone directory for local
    office.)

Telephone Preference Service
6 Reef House
Plantation Wharf
London SW11 3UF

Recommended Further Reading

The BDMA Direct Marketing Desk Reference, ed Sandra Carter and Tessa Kelly (McGraw Hill, 1991)

Commonsense Direct Marketing, Drayton Bird (Kogan Page, 1994)

Cost Effective Direct Marketing, Christian Brann (Collectors' Books Ltd, 1987)

Database Marketing, Robert Shaw and Merlin Stone (Gower, 1996)

Database Marketing & Direct Mail, Robin Fairlie (Kogan Page, 1993)

Direct Marketing – Strategy, Planning, Execution, Edward Nash (McGraw Hill, 1992)

The Essential Guide to Database Marketing, John N. Davies (McGraw Hill, 1992)

Practitioner's Guide to Direct Marketing, Institute of Direct Marketing, 1992

INDEX

above-the-line techniques 11, 12, 27–8, 36
Acorn 83, 119
advertising
  agencies 11
  expenditure 13
  Internet 129, 131–2
  specialists 11
Advertising Standards Authority 97
agency
  best practice guidelines 59–61
  direct mail 55–6
  teamwork communication 61
AHD Property Classification 119, 120
Amstrad 112–13
Apple Tango campaign 92–3
artwork
  production 73
  proofs 74
Association of Household Distributors 119
At Home 27
Audited Bureau of Circulation (ABC) 120

BBC 135
below-the-line techniques 27–8
blood donors, case history 98–9
BMRB 96
British Code of Advertising Practice 79
British Telecommunications (BT) 93–4, 104
brochure/catalogue 66
budget
  allocation 34–7
  limitation 36–7
  setting 57
budgeting/financial control 61
budgets
  business-to-business sector 12
business lists 80–1
Business-to-Business Direct Mail Qualitative Survey 68

Business-to-Business Direct Mail Trends Survey 40
business-to-business sector
  budgets 12
  communication 16–17
  direct mail 39–42, 45–50
  mail order 112
  telemarketing 105, 106

cable television 23, 93
catalogue/brochure 66
CD-i 133, 134
CD-Rom 18, 88, 133, 134
CD technology 133–4
Channel 4 23, 93–4, 104
cinema 26–7
communication
  effectiveness 33
  mix 11–12, 51, 56, 100–1
  objectives 34
  options 34
  packages 27–8
  target customer 34
  tools 128–35
    competition 33–4
    quantitative comparison 33
    successful 33
  with agency 61
communications
  timing 34
competition
  communication tools 33–4
competition-based sales promotion 67
computer-based technology 16
Computer Marketing Technologies (CMT) 82
computer
  networking 22
  systems 134

consumer
  letterbox 42–3
  lists 80
  sector
    direct mail 39, 41–2, 46–8
copywriter/art director team 65
costs
  direct mail 75–6
'costs per thousand' (CPT) 33, 36
creative
  brief
    typical headings 63–4
  material
    analysis in test markets 124–5
    development research 122–4
  package 15, 58
    assessment and approval 72
    direct mail 63–76
    production process 64–8, 72–6
    timing plans 63
creativity 11
customer
  behaviour
    reaction to change 33
  perceptions
    current and future change 33
  response 31
    optimisation 36

data
  handling 21
  manipulation 87
  matching 88–9
Data Protection Act 79, 84–5, 87
Data Protection Principles 85
Data Protection Registrar 84–5
databases
  building 130–1
  compilation and management
    techniques 15, 86–7
  interpretation 89
  maintenance 88–9
  management 87–90
  multi-merge 90
  predictive compilation 89–90
  response information 58
  setting up 57
datacard 79, 84
Datamonitor Publications 12
de-duplication 88–9
Define 83, 119
dialogue 10–11, 36, 47, 66
Direct Line Insurance 93

direct mail 14–16
  agency 59–61
  attitudes 46
  business-to-business sector 39–42,
    45–50
  campaign
    elements 65–8
    objectives 56–7
    organisation 51–62
  consumer sector 41–2, 46–8
  costs 75–6
  creative package 63–76
  definition 38
  enclosing and mailing 74–5
  envelope 65–6
  growth rates 38–9
  initiating/briefing internally 52
  intrusion of privacy 46–7
  issues to be resolved 51
  letter 65
  marketing department responsibility 52
  methodology 47
  'opt-out' boxes 46–7
  optimising external working
    relationships 60–2
  perceived benefits 48
  planning
    ahead 60
    procedures 56–8
  producing and controlling
    by agency 55–6
    by mix of freelance and in-house 54–5
    in-house 54
  producing the work 53–6
  production guidelines 58–9
  questionnaire 66
  receipt 47
  response mechanism 66
  satisfaction levels on responding to 47
  specialist responsibility 52–3
  target identification and access 57
  timing 60
  unsolicited 47
  who uses? 39–42
  written brief 58–9
Direct Mail Information Service 14, 40,
    45–7
direct marketing
  background 9
  definition 10
  expenditure 12–13
  exploratory stage 19
  field covered 15

future 11–12
long-term
    approach 20
    benefits 10
new approach 18–19
potential 10
reappraisal 36
recommended approach 19–20
specific functions 36
techniques 14–15
tools 14–20
who uses? 14
Direct Marketing Association (DMA) 13,
    100
    best practice guidelines 59–61
    Code of Practice 79, 106
    membership 14
    warranty 79–80
Direct Marketing Association Research
    Centre 38
Direct Marketing Solutions 104
direct response advertising 16, 22, 91–9
    and integrated communication
        strategies 92
    and telemarketing 91–2
    expenditure estimates 91
    media-based 91
    published media 95–7
    radio 97–9
    response rates 104
    television 92–5
direct selling 17, 113–15
    growth
        areas 115
        rates 114
    main methods 114
door-to-door 18, 38, 117–21
    as communication medium 15, 118
    benefits 117–18
    campaign issues 118
    costs 121
    delivery
        methods 119–20
        validation checks 120–1
    distribution channels 119
    material for 118
    solus or shared 120
    target audience 119

Flanagans 115
free newspapers 120
freepost mechanism 66

geodemographics 82–3, 119
gimmick 67
grocery delivery services 115
group discussions 123

Heinz 27
home shopping services 134–5
    future developments 115–16
Hoseasons Holidays 95

ICD 82
independent radio 26
integrated communications
    plan 27–37, 67
    strategy 29–30
        agency 28
        and direct response advertising 92
        development 30
        direct marketing 35–7
        elements 30–5
        outline headings 35
interactive
    kiosks 134
    television 134–5
Internet 18, 22, 128–33
    advertising 129, 131–2
    and direct marketing 130
    basic rules 129
    history 129
    mail order 131
    points to avoid 132–3

junk mail 9–10

laser printing 74
letterfoot 68
letterhead 68
letters
    guidelines on producing 68–71
    headline 69
    layout 70
    optimum length 69
    personalised 74
    printing 70
    PS 70
    sub-headings 70
    welcoming greeting 69
    writing style 71
lifestyle information 81–2
list
    brokers 79
    managers 78
    owners 78

mail order 17
  business-to-business sector 112
  distribution system 113
  growth rates 112–13
  Internet 131
  leading houses and catalogues 110–11
  market shares 111
  new generation 112–13
  origins 109
  traditional 109–12
  upmarket and specialist products 112
Mail Order Protection Scheme 97
mailing lists 78–87
  bought-in external 78–86
  business 78
  circulation 78
  compiled 78
  copyright 84
  costs 84
  datacard 79, 84
  electronic format 83
  formats 83
  in-house generated 78, 86–7
  information sources 78–9
  legal controls 84
  paper based format 83
  responders 78
  seed names 84
  self-regulation 84
  sources 47, 78
  suitability 80
  usage rights 84
  virtual format 83
Mailing Preference Service (MPS) 79,
    85–7
mailsort 75, 80, 88
marketing department 11
  responsibility in direct mail 52
Mars Snickers 130
Media & Marketing Europe 11
media-based direct response advertising 16
media fragmentation 23–7
men's press 25
Mintel 96
Mosaic 83, 119

National Change of Address File
    (NCOA) 88
national press 24–5
NDL Information 82
network selling 114
neural networks 89
new media 18

newspaper sales 24
Next Directory 112
novelty/gimmick 67

objective 31
'one stop shop' approach 28

Pareto principle 90
party plan 114
Peapod 115
Periodical Publishers Association 97
post-campaign analysis 125–7
Post Office 75
Post Office Redirection Service 88
postcodes 88
posters 26
press advertising
  direct response 95–7
price list 66–7
printing
  direct mail 74
priorities 31
profile generation 81–2

qualitative research 122–4
quantitative research 122–4
Quantum 93
questionnaires 123
QVC 93

radio
  direct response advertising 97–9
  network 26
Radio Times 25
Reader's Digest 67
regression analysis 82, 89
relationship building 11
research techniques 122–7
Royal Mail 119–20
  Consumer Panel 42
  Postcode Address File (PAF) 88

Sainsbury's 115
sales promotion item 67
satellite television 23, 93
Scottish Gourmet 96–7
Sears Roebuck Corporation 109
sensitive areas 32
Shoppers Express 115
single level selling 114
Sky Television 135
Snickers Megabite 130
software developments 21–2

Somerfield 115
Soundex 89
standard industrial code (SIC) 81
statistical models 82
stuffers 67–8
Superprofiles 83, 119

take away food delivery service 115–16
target
    audiences 36–7
    customer 32
        communication 34
teamwork
    communication with agency 61
technological developments 21–2
telecommunications 16
telemarketing 16–17, 22, 100–8
    advantages 104
    and direct response advertising 91–2
    automatic call-handling system 103
    business-to-business sector 105, 106
    capital investment 101
    customer care lines 107
    expenditure 100
    growth rates 100
    inbound 100, 101–4
        bureau versus in-house 102–4
        costs 102–4
        fully automated 101–2

guideline information brief 103
        key elements 102
        lost calls 104
        operator based 101–2
    in-house sourced 100–1
    outbound 100, 104–7
        bureau versus in-house 105–6
        costs 105–6
        guidelines 106–7
telephone
    call handling 22
    numbers 88
    system 101
Telephone Preference Service 107–8
television 23–4
    direct response advertising 93–5
    interactive 134–5
    listings magazines 25
Tesco 115, 131
test marketing 124–5
theme/mission statement 30–1
TV Times 25
TVAM (now GMTV) 23

Verified Free Newspaper Distribution
    (VFD) 120
Viking Direct 113

women's press 25